AUSTRALIAN HOMESCHOOLING SERIES

Successful English 8A

Years 8-10

CORONEOS PUBLICATIONS

Item No 562

This book is available from recognised booksellers or contact:

Coroneos Publications

Telephone: (02) 9838 9265   **Facsimile:** (02) 9838 8982
Business Address: 2/195 Prospect Highway Seven Hills 2147
Website: www.coroneos.com.au
E-mail: info@fivesenseseducation.com.au

Item # 562
Successful English 8A
by Valerie Marett
First published 2017

ISBN: 978-1-922034-43-4
© Valerie Marett

Writing Checklist—refer to during each writing exercise

1. **Identify the genre or style of writing required:**
   - Is it a report, a story, a poem etc? Make sure you understand what is required for each genre.

2. **Story Writing, Report Writing, Autobiography, Biography:**
   - Make sure you understand your topic.
   - Ask any of the following questions that apply:
      a. **Who** is the story about?
      b. **What** is the plot or main event in the story? Always jot down any ideas you have on a spare sheet of paper. Never try to keep them in your head.
      c. **Where** is it set?
      d. **When** does it take place?
      e. **How?** The process that was undertaken.
      f. **Characters:** Who is the main character or characters? Are there other important characters? Outline them.

3. **For all types of writing:**
   - **Jot** down any ideas on a sheet of paper.
   - **Read** them through and **number** them in the order you wish to use them. **Cross out** any that are not appropriate.
   - Create an **outline** from these notes.
   - **Expand** your ideas by creating sentences using the ideas, but still following the sequence in your outline.
   - You must have a **beginning**, a **middle** and a **conclusion** or **end**.

4. **Check your work for the following:**
   - Are there at least two sentences in a paragraph?
   - Do your sentences begin in different ways for interest and are they of different length?
   - Do your sentences build on the previous ones and are they clear?
   - Have you spelt correctly?
   - Is all your writing in the first person, second person, etc.?
   - Are you writing in the past, present or future tense correctly?
   - Have you used correct capitalization and punctuation?
   - Does your beginning or introduction catch the reader's attention?
   - If you are writing a story or a biography, have you developed your character sufficiently?
   - If you are writing a story does it reach a climax before the final ending?
   - Have you brought your writing to a logical conclusion or have you left it hanging?
   - If there is a dialogue, do you have quotation marks around the conversation and does each new conversation begin on another line?
   - If you are writing a report have you included all the relevant facts?

- Each time you had a new idea did you start a new paragraph?
- Can you add adjectives or adverbs that will make the writing more vivid? (Don't over do it.)
- No sentences are begun with "but", "and" or "however".
- Have some words been used too frequently? Use a thesaurus to find words that could be used instead.
- Is your handwriting legible?

Writing A Letter

- Does your writing have a **heading**? (The address of the person writing the letter. Commas are used to separate parts of the address.)
- Have you included the **date**?
- Have you chosen a suitable **greeting**? For example, you might use "Dear Jill," to greet a friend but a business letter would begin more formally, "Dear Mr Fisher."
- Check the length of the **body** of the letter. If you are writing to a friend the length does not matter, but if you are writing a business letter it is important to keep it brief and to the point.
- Choose a suitable **closing**. A letter to a friend might end "Your friend, John," but a business letter should be more formally, e.g., "Yours faithfully, John Smith."
- Is the **envelope** addressed correctly? The sender's address should be in the top left hand corner. The address direction should be in the middle of the envelope. There should be no commas in the address as this confuses the sorting machine.

Advertisement

Many of the suggestions already given will apply but in addition the following should be considered:

- Can people reading your advertisement see clearly what you are selling?
- Have you restricted the wording without losing the message? If there are too many words a potential customer will lose interest and you will lose a sale.
- Have you added pictures to make the advertisement attractive? If the product you are selling is good you will not need gimmicks, free gifts or other offers to sell it. If you are competing with a large market look for another item to sell. You can not compete with large manufacturers. The small business does best in a niche market.

Procedures: Writing Instructions

Many of the suggestions already given will apply but in addition the following should be considered:

- Are the instructions clear? Is it possible to follow the instructions you have given? Get a friend to try to follow the instructions exactly as they are written.
- Are the instructions concise?
- Would illustrations or examples help the reader? For example, if the instruction is to make a craft item then illustrations would help. If the instruction is in, for example, a maths book, then several worked problems might aid the reader.

Reviewing Plural Nouns

Basic Rules N.B. There are some exceptions.

● **The plural form of most nouns is created by adding s,** e.g., snake, snakes.

● **Words that end in –ch, x or s require an -es to make them plural,** e.g., box, boxes.

● **Some nouns are irregular,** e.g., woman, women.

● **Some nouns retain their Greek or Latin form,** e.g., nucleus, nuclei.

● **a few words only exist in the plural,** e.g., mathematics, cattle.

Write the plural form of each noun listed below.

1. mosquito _____	2. fly _____
3. gallery _____	4. quiz _____
5. fungus _____	6. atlas _____
7. storey _____	8. bench _____
9. pliers _____	10. vertex _____
11. index _____	12. symphony _____
13. mouse _____	14. volcano _____
15. legislation _____	16. potato _____
17. knife _____	18. gulf _____
19. larva _____	20. synopsis _____
21. dictionary _____	22. louse _____
23. ovum _____	24. tax _____
25. roof _____	26. cactus _____
27. daughter-in-law _____	28. church _____
29. bacterium _____	30. zoo _____
31. tomato _____	32. cattle _____

© Valerie Marett
Coroneos Publications

Australian Homeschooling #562
Successful English 8A

Review of Nouns

Six things to remember about nouns

- They can be singular or plural., e.g., gas, gases
- They can be common or proper nouns, e.g., car (common); Perth (proper).
- They can be masculine, feminine, neuter or common gender, e.g., boy (masculine); girl (feminine); rock (neuter); people, sheep (common gender).
- They can be abstract or concrete, e.g., bricks, rain, glass (concrete); bravery, despair, pride, happiness (abstract).
- Concrete nouns may be collective, e.g., a mob of kangaroos.
- They may be the subject or object of the verb.

A. Use a collective noun to complete each phrase below.

1. a _____ of directors   2. a _____ of puppies

3. a _____ of would-be spectators

4. a _____ of labourers   5. a _____ of replies

6. a _____ of violinists   7. a _____ of runs in cricket

B. Make abstract nouns of each word below by adding —sion, —ance, —cy , —tion or ——ness.

1. conscious   _____   2. radiant   _____

3. intrude _____   4. distort   _____

5. accurate   _____   6. allude   _____

C. Write the correct abstract now to fit each definition below.

1. the state of being alert and watchful   _____

2. the act of coming to an end   _____

3. the act of sailing a ship   _____

4. the act of thrusting oneself in where not wanted   _____

5. the act of giving help or approval   _____

A. Some nouns change their form according to gender. Match each of the masculine nouns with their feminine form.

1. boar _____

2. bachelor _____

3. buck _____

4. stallion _____

5. heir _____

6. waiter _____

7. ram _____

8. duke _____

9. gander _____

10. bridegroom _____

Most nouns name things that are neither male or female, e.g., house, grass, lake, pen. These are said to be neuter gender.

A few nouns may be both male and female, e.g., people, poultry, children, sheep. These nouns are said to be common gender.

The pronouns you, we, us, they, them can also be common gender.

B. Complete the following with nouns of common gender.

1. the noun that includes men, women and children _____

2. the noun that includes hens, drakes and turkeys _____

3. the noun that includes mares and stallions _____

C. Write a noun listing a small quantity of something, e.g., a small quantity of wood is a splinter.

1. a _____ of dust

2. a _____ of hair

3. a _____ of rain

4. a _____ of salt

5. a _____ of bread

6. a _____ of air

D. Rewrite the sentence replacing the underlined part of the sentence with a noun.

1. The train approached <u>the place where two lines meet.</u>

_____

2. Who would win the election was a subject for <u>making guesses.</u>

_____

The Rise of the Feudal System

You will remember that Charles Mantel needed an effective army to cope with the Moslems and Saxons and also to put an end to the continual revolts of rival families. He enlisted able warriors and made them swear absolute fidelity to him, making them his vassi dominici. To each he gave an estate large enough to support the vassal as long as he remained loyal. He also forced the Church to grant benefices to men on condition they serve as soldiers. While in theory these men were vassals of the Church they were really under control of Charles.

His son Pepin continued creating vassals and drove the Moslems back over the Pyrenees and forced the Duke of Bavaria to acknowledge his lordship. Charlemagne, who succeeded Pepin, beat the Saxons and brought in French counts giving them land which they had to keep order. He used his cavalry to invade Bavaria, remove the Duke and divide up the land into counties. The land here and in Lombardy, which he also conquered, was administered by Counts, while the border areas were controlled by Margraves. Although he kept his nobles under control, after his death there was continued civil war and anarchy existed.

To add to this general confusion there were Viking, Moslem and Magyar raiders. No village, cathedral city or monastic establishment was safe unless protected by soldiers.

In this state of anarchy the ordinary freeman had two choices: he could become a soldier or sink to the status of serf. A serf was the lowest member of society who was attached to a lord and required to supply labour in return for certain legal or customary rights.

So the Kings, their officials, the great landlords, and even important vassi dominici, sought armed followers to aid them in war. Every man who had more land than he needed gave benefices to soldiers who became his vassals. Landlords began to seek protection of even more powerful men. When a vassi dominicus found the King could no longer protect him he gave his allegiance to someone else, perhaps a count. He surrendered his land to a more powerful man than himself, received it from him as a benefice and became his vassal.

During the ninth century there developed a hierarchy of lords and vassals. The simple knight had a small area of land and enough labour to support his family. In turn he was a vassal of a larger land owner, who in turn, would be a vassal of a mightier man, perhaps a Count. The Count might be a vassal of a Duke or the King.

As a result the relationship between lords and vassals changed. The greatest change was that the benefice was no longer revocable, or at best a lifetime grant, but an hereditary one. By the tenth century most benefices were hereditary and somewhere about this time the benefice became known as a feudum or fief, an estate held from a superior lord on condition homage and service were performed. The estate or manor was know as a fief or fiefdom.

A. Definitions: find a word in the text that fits each definition below.

1. an estate held from a superior lord on condition homage and service were performed

   _____

2. a warrior who swore absolute fidelity to someone in return for an estate

   _____

3. the strict carrying out of promises, duties, etc.

   _____

4. a position given by the Church providing a living in return for service and loyalty

   _____

5. the condition of society without government or law

   _____

6. a system of graded ranks within society

   _____

7. able to be taken back

   _____

8. the lowest member of a society who was attached to a lord and required to provide labour in return for certain rights

   _____

B. Answer these questions from the text on page 8. Always answer in sentences.

1. Who was the first person who made his warriors vassi dominici? Why did he do this?

   _____

   _____

2. What happened after the death of Charlemagne?

   _____

3. Think. Where did the Viking, Moslem and Magyar Raiders come from?

   _____

   _____

4. What were the only two choices available to a free man?

   _____

5. What was the greatest change that developed in this early feudal system?

   _____

English Poetry Through the Ages:
Anglo-Norman Period and Early Middle Ages

The Norman conquest of England in 1066 led to a rapid decline of the Anglo-Saxon language. As the invaders spoke French this became the standard language of the courts and polite society. Gradually the French became integrated into the English language, but it was not until the fourteenth century that major works of English literature began again to appear. Among these were "Sir Gawain and the Green Knight" and also works by Geoffrey Chaucer.

"Sir Gawain and the Green Knight" was written in the dialect of Middle English about the fourteenth century, but has been translated into a slightly more modern form below so you can understand it.

Read the extract from "Sir Gawain and the Green Knight". This extract deals with King Arthur and Camelot. Notice how the language still differs from today. In the section you will read it is Christmas at King Arthur's Court and all the knights and ladies have gathered to celebrate with a feast.

In the rest of the segment King Arthur refuses to eat until he has witnessed something marvellous or heard a great adventure story. Luckily, just as everyone is sitting down to eat, a mysterious, gigantic stranger with emerald-green skin and clothed in green bursts into the hall on a gigantic green horse and carrying an elaborately-decorated axe.

The Green Knight announces that he's come to test the honor of the legendary Knights of the Round Table, and proposes a game: he will withstand a single axe-blow from the hands of one knight, as long as that knight agrees to meet him in a year and a day to receive an axe-blow in return. No-one responds and the Green Knight mocks them. King Arthur is about to accept the challenge when his nephew, Sir Gawain accepts.

Many adventures befall Sir Gawain before he finally finds the Green Knight and discovers his identity and the reason for the challenge.

> At Camelot lay the King, all on Christmas-tide,
> With many a lovely lord, and gallant knight beside,
> And of the Table Round did the rich brotherhood
> High revel hold aright, and mirthful was their mood:
> Oft-times on tourney bent those gallants sought the field,
> And gentle knights in joust would shiver spear and shield;
> Anon would seek the court for sport and carol gay—
> For fifteen days told the feast was held away,
> With all the meat and mirth that men might well devise,
> Right glorious was the glee that rang in riotous wise
>
> With all this world's weal they dwelt, those gallant guests;
> For Christ no braver knights had faced or toil or strife,

No fairer ladies e'er had drawn the breath of life
And he, the comliest king that e'er held court, forsooth,
For all this goodly folk were e'en in their first youth
　　　　And still
　　　　The happiest under heaven
　　　　A king of stalwart will,
　　　　'T were hard with them to even
　　　　Another host on hill!

Complete the following:

1. A couplet is a pair of successive lines of verse, usually rhyming, and having the same metre. The poem is written in couplets and many of the poem's lines rhyme. Write 3 examples of these rhyming couplets.

   _____

   _____

2. Explain these words:

   a. **tourney:** _____

   b. **joust:** _____

   _____

   c. **comliest:** _____

   d. **glee:** _____

3. How long did the Christmas feast last?

   _____

Geoffrey Chaucer, known as the Father of English literature, is considered the greatest English poet in the Middle Ages. He lived in the late fourteenth century and served as a diplomat in the Court of Edward III. It is difficult to know when he started writing poetry but he best known for his Canterbury Tales.

The tales are told by a group of pilgrims as they travel together on a journey from Southwark to the Shrine of Thomas Becket at Canterbury Cathedral. They agree that the person who tells the best story has a free meal in Southwark on their return.

England at this time had survived through the Black Death, which had wiped out half of the population and there had been a rise in the lower trade classes that had unsettled the nobility. The characters in this poem represent a cross view of society at the time they include the Narrator (Chaucer,) A Wife of Bath, A Knight, a Squire, a Monk, a Prioress, a Miller, a Friar, a Pardoner—a person who granted "indulgences" in exchange for a gift to the Church, and a Clerk. Chaucer originally intended there to be 120 tales but ended with 24.

Read the Prologue to the Canterbury Tales written below. The first four verses are written in Middle English, which you may understand better if you read it aloud; section two has been translated into more modern language. Notice how much our language has changed over time.

Whan that Aprille with his shoures sote
The droghte of Marche hath perced to the rote,
And battled every veyne in swich licour,
Of which vertu engendred is the flour;

When the sweet showers of April follow March,
Piercing its drought down to the roots that parch,
Bathing each vein in such a flow of power
That a new strength is engendered in the flower—
When, with gentle warmth, the west-wind's breath
Awakes in every wood and barren heath
The tender foliage, when the vernal sun
Has half his course within the Ram to run—
When the small birds are making melodies,
Sleeping all night (they say) with open eyes
(For Nature so within their bosom rages)—
Then people long to go on pilgrimages,
And palmers wander to the strangest strands
For famous shrines, however far the lands.
Especially from every shire's end
Of England's length to Canterbury they wend
Seeking the martyr, holiest and blest
Who helped them, healed their ills, and gave them rest
Befell that in that season, on a day
In Southwark, at the Tabard, as I lay
Ready to start upon my pilgrimage
To Canterbury full of devout homage,
There came at nightfall to that hostelry
Some nine and twenty in a company
Of sundry persons who had chanced to fall
In fellowship, and pilgrims were they all
That toward Canterbury town would ride……………...

Answer the following questions:

1. What was a pilgrimage as described in the poem?

   _____

2. Why did pilgrims usually travel together in a group?

   _____

3. What season was it? How do you know?

   _____

   _____

4. Note that rhyming couplets are again used. They are very common in poetry. Give two examples of these rhyming couplets.

_____

5. Look back at the original language of Chaucer. Find a word from the more modern version that matches each word below. Note that some of the words, when pronounced, sound the same even though the spelling is different. Other words have changed dramatically.

a. shoures _____   b. sote _____

c. droghte _____   d. rote _____

e. veyne _____   f. flour _____

Research, then write a one page summary on either of the following topics. Follow all the conventions of writing including rough drafts. Do not use slang or text speak. Attach the copy below.

- **King Arthur: who was he and what was the legend surrounding him?**

- **Thomas Becket: who was he, what made him famous and cause pilgrims to visit his tomb?**

_____
_____
_____
_____
_____
_____
_____
_____
_____
_____
_____
_____
_____
_____
_____
_____
_____

© Valerie Marett
Coroneos Publications

Australian Homeschooling #562
Successful English 8A

Using the Correct Ending to a Word

A. Complete each sentence below by adding "—ary" or "—ery". If you aren't sure use a dictionary.

1. The volunt_____ artill_____ group received an hon_____ medal.

2. If the size of your vocabul_____ remains station_____, a diction_____ may be necess_____ to improve it.

3. The brib_____ attempt was written in red ink on blue station_____.

4. People in sedent_____ jobs should have some salut_____ exercise.

5. Flatt_____ is only of second_____ importance.

B. Add "—ceed," "—cede" or "—sede" to the following to form complete words.

1 se_____   2. ac_____   3. ex_____

4. re_____   5. super_____   6. pre_____

7. pro_____   8. con_____   9. suc_____

C. Complete each sentence below by adding "—cy" or "—sy." "—sy" is rare.

1. All the motels have their 'no vacan_____' sign on during the holidays.

2. The firm went into bankrupt_____.

3 John Hus was excommunicated for here_____ before he was burnt at the stake.

4. Some countries still only have a tenper-cent liter_____ rate.

5. Can a democra_____ also be a bureaucra_____?

D. Each sentence below contains the "—efy" or "—ify". Complete by adding "e" or "i" in the space indicated.

1. Should the Executive Council rat__fy the new legislation on offshore mining?

2. The witness is about to test___fy.

3. Unfrozen meat soon putr___fies.

4. Liqu___fied oxygen is used in rockets.

Occupations

Name the person below who......

1. builds with stone _____
2. fits pipes to convey water _____
3. sells flowers for a profit _____
4. sets glass in window-frames _____
5. takes part in competitive physical sport _____
6. engages in the business of selling lollies _____
7. carves and mould figures _____
8. drives a car for a living _____
9. climbs tall buildings to make repairs _____
10. is legally qualified as a lawyer _____

Correct Word

Many mistakes are made in English due to confusing arising from the similarity of sound or appearance of certain words.

Choose the correct word in brackets that means the same as the word or words in the first column. Use a dictionary if necessary

1. to influence (affect, effect) _____
2. important (momentary, momentous) _____
3. clever (ingenuous, ingenious) _____
4. bearing or appearance (mean, mien) _____
5. to go ahead (precede, proceed) _____
6. reference (allusion, illusion) _____
7. despicable (contemptuous, contemptible) _____
8. easy to read (eligible, legible) _____

Review of Verbs

Remember, at its simplest, a verb is a doing, being or having word.

Verbs can be finite or non-finite.

- **A finite verb has a subject and can stand alone, e.g.,** The boy ran away.
- **A non-finite verb can not stand alone, e.g.,** <u>to swim</u> to the other bank.

There are two kinds of non-finite verbs; infinitives and participles.

- **The infinitive verb is a verb without reference to the subject. It cannot act as a complete verb in a sentence. It is often preceded by "to".**
  e.g., I am going <u>to go</u> to the dance

- **There are two kinds of participles: present and past. Both the present and past participles combine with a helping (auxiliary) verb to make a complete verb.**
  e.g., I am dancing on the stage. (present)
  I had danced on stage. (past)

Verbs may be singular or plural.
  e.g., The girl dances. (singular)
  The girls dance. (plural)

Verbs may be present, past or future tense.

Verbs may be transitive or intransitive.

- **Transitive verbs need an object and show the action passing from the subject to something else.** The boy passed the ball to his friend.
- **Intransitive verbs do not have an object,** e.g., The boy shouted loudly.

A Underline the verb or verbs in each sentence below and say what type they are.

1. The paddock gate was broken by a cow. _____

2. People can cause fires by dropping lighted cigarettes.

   _____

3. The car ran into the back of a truck. _____

B. Write the verb. Say if it is transitive or intransitive.

1. The water boiled quickly. _____

2. Write down eight objects _____

3. They sang, in perfect harmony, songs we all knew.

   _____

4. Robert laughed loudly. _____

Identify the noun or nouns and verb or verbs in each sentence below. Write them on the line provided. (You may count pronouns as nouns for this exercise.)

1. Gold was discovered near Kalgoorlie.

   _____

2. Two cars came up the hill and over the crest.

   _____

3. A wreath of flowers was placed on the school's war memorial.

   _____

4. You know he and I are close friends.

   _____

5. The spectator screamed with delight.

   _____

6. Having kissed mother goodbye, I hurried on my way.

   _____

7. The postman opened the gate.

   _____

8. It is raining heavily but you must still go to school.

   _____

9. Mt Kosciusko is often visited by tourists and skiers who like rugged scenery.

   _____

10. Krystal said that she had to draw a map of Australia.

   _____

11. Our new teacher is a very charming person.

   _____

12. A few of the bushland creatures were darting in and out of the scrub.

   _____

13. I still like to drink hot tea in summer.

   _____

Feudalism: How it Functioned

Society took the form of a pyramid with the King at the apex, who in theory, had sovereignty of all persons. When he granted land to the great nobles he invested them with sovereign rights so that each Tenant in Chief became a sovereign in his own domain. The Tenants in Chief in turn granted land to other tenants. This process, known as sub-infeudation, could be carried on to almost any degree. When the king called on his Tenants in Chief they had to appear with a fully armed army, so, to distribute the cost, it was necessary to have lesser tenants who would also have to produce forces when called upon.

At the base of the pyramid were about 80%—90% of the people who could not fight as they had no horses or weapons. These were the serfs; men who were originally free with a customary right to the land on which they lived, but who had lost their freedom under feudal law and had become bound to the land. If the land was sold, they were sold with it. They had cottages and a few acres consisting of narrow stirps of land scattered about great open fields. They served their masters by working in the fields, building his bridges, mending his roads, guarding his cattle and producing his food. In return it was his duty to protect them from other lords or marauding robbers. In times of trouble the serfs withdrew into the castle hold.

There were certain obligations on the part of the vassal and his immediate overlord. These were worked out independently by each lord and his vassals, and the vassals were far stronger than the overlords who were utterly helpless if their vassals turned against them.

The vassals basic purpose was military service. Originally the amount of service that could be demanded was unlimited, but later forty days a year became the maximum. They were also obliged to attend the lord's Court when summoned. The lord would seek counsel from them on any question that was of interest to the fief and those assembled decided any disputes.

A feudal vassal also had to pay relief to his lord. This changed so that the money was paid when an heir succeeded to a fief. By the twelfth century it was paid in money rather than kind and was probably the revenue from the fief for one year. Another obligation was known as "aid." When a lord needed extra money he naturally sought it from his vassals. The vassals were expected to contribute towards the knighting of the Lord's eldest son or the wedding of his daughter. They had to help if their Lord wanted to go on a Crusade or build a castle or if he had to be ransomed.

In addition there was the duty of offering hospitality to the Lord. The Lord, with his retinue, could visit a vassal a certain number of times each year and the vassal had to entertain him.

In return the lord was expected to protect his vassal and his fief from all foes and was bound to give him justice in Vassals Court. He was also bound to respect the family and personal interests of his vassals. If the lord failed the vassal could "defy" him and declare war against him.

A. Answer these questions:

1. List the societal order under feudalism.

   _____

2. What were the responsibilities of the Tennant-in-Chief and vassals? (Don't miss any.)

   _____

   _____

   _____

   _____

   _____

3. What were the responsibilities of the king or any overlord?

   _____

   _____

4. What were the serfs duties and rights?

   _____

   _____

   _____

5. Do you think, from reading the text, that this worked well?

   _____

   _____

B. Word knowledge: find a word in the text that means the following:

1. money paid by a vassal to an over-lord   _____

2. the highest point   _____

3. an area of territory owned or controlled by a particular lord   _____

4. a body of servants accompanying an important person   _____

C. Research:

Knights of this period had a code of chivalry that they were expected to live by. On becoming a knight they took an oath to follow this code. Discover what was contained in the code. Make a scroll listing the code.

English Poetry Through the Ages:
Renaissance England & Elizabethan Poets

The Renaissance period in England was from 1509 to 1660. The introduction of moveable-block printing by Caxton in 1474 led to the more rapid dissemination of new or recently discovered writers. In addition the writings of Thomas Moore and Thomas Elyot helped bring the ideas and attitudes associated with new learning to an English audience.

In addition the establishment of the Church of England in 1535 accelerated the process of questioning the Catholic world view that had previously dominated intellectual life. In addition long-distance exploratory sea voyages help bring a new understanding of the universe.

Thomas Wyatt was the most famous poet of the Renaissance period. He was an ambassador to Italy and France for King Henry VIII and was therefore exposed to other forms of poetry. He is believed to be the first poet to have written sonnets in English. Most of the poems of this time were love poems.

A sonnet shows two differing things to a reader to communicate something about them. Study the poem below by Thomas Wyatt carefully.

Description of the Contrarious Passions in a Lover

I find no peace and all my war is done;
I fear and hope, I burn and freeze like ice;
I fly aloft and yet I can not arise;
And nought I have, and all the world I seize on,
That locks nor loseth, holdeth me in prison,
And holds me not, yet can I scape no wise:
Nor letteth me live, nor die at my devise,
And yet of death it giveth me occasion.
Without eye I see; without tongue I plain:
I wish to perish yet I ask for health;
I love another, and I hate myself;
I feed me in sorrow, and laugh in all my pain.
Lo, thus displeaseth me both death and life;
And my delight is causer of this strife.

Answer these questions:

1. Go through the poem again and underline the differing things. List 2 of them below.

_____

_____

2. The English in this poem differs slightly from the English used today and is much more easily understood than the English in Chaucer's time. Write the equivalent in modern language of each word below.

a. nought _____   b. scape _____

c. no wise _____   d. at my devise _____

e. causer _____   f. strife _____

3. Explain briefly what the poem is speaking of.

_____

_____

The Elizabethan period lasted from 1558 -1603. It was characterised by the introduction and adaptation of themes, models and verse forms from the European traditions and classic literature, the emergence of courtly poetry, often centred around the monarch. In addition many poets wrote songs as well as poems. Shakespeare produced his plays during this period and also wrote some sonnets.

Read the following poems by William Shakespeare.

Winter

When icicles hang by the wall
And Dick the shepherd blows his nail;
And Tom bears log into the hall,
And milk comes frozen home in pail;
When blood is nipt, and ways be foul,
Then nightly sings the staring owl
Tu-whoo!
To-whit, Tu-whoo! A merry note!
While greasy Joan doth keel the pot.

When all about the wind doth blow,
And coughing drowns the parson's saw,
And birds sit brooding in the snow,
And Mariam's nose looks red and raw;
When roasted crabs hiss in the bowl—
Then nightly sings the starting owl
Tu-whoo!
To-whit, Tu-whoo! A merry note!
While greasy Joan doth keel the pot.

This poem was may have been written about a dear friend or Elizabeth 1. She is reputed to have been jealous of other women.

Eternal Summer

Shall I compare thee to a summer's day?
Thou art more lovely and more temperate;
Rough winds do shake the darling buds of May,
And summer's lease hath all too short a date:
Sometime too hot the eye of heaven shines,
And often is his gold complexion dimmed:
And every fair from fair sometimes declines,
By chance, or nature's changing course, untrimmed:

But thy eternal summer shall not fade
Nor lose the possession of that fair thou owest;
Nor shall Death brag thou wanderest in his shade
When in eternal lines to time thou growest.
So long as men can breathe, or eye can see
So lives this, and this gives life to thee.

Answer these questions:

1. Re-read the poem "Winter" on page 21. Describe what the weather was like in England in winter. Give examples of the images in the poem that substantiate your argument.

   _____

   _____

   _____

2. Explain the following: "when blood is nipt and ways be foul."

   _____

   _____

3. Write the equivalent word or phrase in modern language.

   a. keel the pot _____

   b. the parson's saw _____

   c. birds sit brooding _____

4. Note how many alternate lines rhyme. Give an example.

   _____

5. Re-read the poem "Eternal Summer" on page 22. What time of year is it? (Remember the poem is set in England and their seasons are opposite to ours.) Explain your answer.

_____

_____

_____

6. What is the name for the type of rhyming in the poem?

_____

7. "When in eternal lines thou growest" is a grafted metaphor. Give an explanation for the meaning of this and the next two lines?

_____

8. Explain the following terms:

    a. the summer's lease _____

    b. temperate _____

    c. the eye of heaven _____ .

9. What has been personified in the poem?

_____

10. What is the theme of this poem?

_____

Note the progress through the poem as the poet changes from praise of a friend, or the Queen, into making them a perfect being and a standard to live up to.

Research and Write:

Elizabeth 1 was a great Queen. She was the daughter of Henry VIII. Explain briefly the following:

- Henry's marriage to Anne Boleyn and why it occurred. Hint: Henry needed a son. Civil war had resulted from the reign of the only other Queen, Matilda.
- the obstacles that she had to overcome before she became Queen.
- Her achievements during her reign
- Her relationship with Spain
- Explorations under her reign
- Her legacy
- Your conclusion on whether or not she achieved greatness.

French Words and Phrases Used in English

English contains many words of French origin that have become Anglicised over the years, e.g., machine, force, police, routine.

Match the definition to the correct word or phrase in the box. Learn what you do not know.

> resume; tete-a-tete; applique; nom de plume; boutique;
> a la carte; fait accompli; repertoire; au fait; debut; vinaigrette;
> façade; a la mode; sabotage; premiere; bon appetit

1. individual dishes ordered rather than a fixed price meal. _____

2. a fake persona _____

3. author's pseudonym _____

4. a body of items regularly performed _____

5. subversive destruction _____

6. an accomplished fact; something that has already
   happened and is unlikely to be repeated _____

7. an intimate get together or private conversation
   between two people _____

8. salad dressing of oil and vinegar _____

9. an inlaid or decorative feature _____

10. fashionable _____

11. a clothing store, usually selling designer rather than
    mass produced clothes _____

12. first public performance of an entertainment
    personality or group _____

13. first performance of a play or film _____

14. a document listing one's qualifications for a job _____

15. being conversant in or with, or instructed in or with _____

16. good appetite; enjoy your meal _____

Suffixes

A. Choose an adjective from the box to fit each definition below. Underline its suffix.

> skittish, negligible, prostrate, transitory, insular, vindictive, dilatory, derogatory

1. tending to delay _____

2. passing soon, fleeting _____

3. given to take revenge _____

4. rather excitable and capricious _____

5. showing an unfavourable opinion; belittling _____

6. unimportant enough to be neglected _____

7. lying flat with face down _____

8. narrow minded _____

B. Choose a noun from the box to fit each definition below. Underline its suffix.

> appropriateness, vacancy, egotist, slovenliness, predecessor, emulation, atheist, philatelist, successor

1. a person holding a position before another person _____

2. a person who thinks and talks about themselves too much _____

3. a person who takes a place left by another _____

4. a person who collects stamps _____

5. the quality of being very untidy _____

6. the state of being empty _____

7. the state of imitating someone successfully _____

8. the state of being suitable to the occasion _____

9. a person who believes there is no God _____

Review of Adjectives

Adjectives may be divided into six main classes:

a. **Descriptive:** these describe the way the person or thing is named by a noun, e.g., bright sunlight, creaky stairs, pretty girl.

b. **Demonstrative: this, that, these, those** demonstrate or point out which and are called demonstrative adjectives.

c. **Interrogative: which** and **what** when they qualify nouns are interrogative adjectives, e.g., Which cake would you prefer?

d. **Possessive: my, his, her, its, our, your, there are** possessive adjectives, e.g., My lunch is here and your lunch is over there.

e. **Numerical:** these are cardinal and ordinal numbers when they qualify nouns, e.g., sixth child, four cats.

f. **Distributive: each, every, either neither** are distributive adjectives when they qualify a noun, e.g., Either book may be given to each pupil.

B. **Look at each sentence below. Say which class each of the underlined adjectives belongs. State the noun it qualifies.**

1. The **fifth** candidate on the ballot was **my** cousin. He always knew how to answer every question put to him.

   _____

2. **Neither** boy knew **what** homework he had to do.

   _____

3. **These** loaves are not as **fresh** as they were.

   _____

4. On **this** page you have made **two serious** errors that need your attention before the **next** publication of the book.

   _____

5. In **which** month do we get the **finest** weather?

   _____

6. Is the **last** question the **sixth** on the list?

   _____

Rewrite the sentences below, substituting a single adjective from the box for each underlined phrase. Be careful, you may need to rearrange the sentence.
For example: We noticed several houses **in which nobody lives.**
We noticed several uninhabited houses.

---

immortal, unprecedented, blank, glimmering, obsolete, improvident, unassuming, uninhabited, impromptu, garrulous, gargantuan

1. He was shipwrecked on an island **on which no one lived.**

   _____

2. It was an event **for which there was no previous example.**

   _____

3. She made a speech **for which she could not prepare.**

   _____

4. **Of a thriftless nature,** he did not provide for the future.

   _____

5. He appetite was **enormous, like the giant's in Jack and the Bean Stalk.**

   _____

6. He was a child **who made little of his accomplishments.**

   _____

7. There was only a light **that shone feverishly and intermittently.**

   _____

8. The work of Shakespeare is likely to be **famous for all times.**

   _____

9. Old people sometimes become **too fond of talking idly.**

   _____

10. I took a sheet of paper **on which nothing had been written.**

   _____

11. Wooden warships are **no longer used.**

   _____

Agriculture in Medieval Times

The bulk of the population in the tenth and eleventh century were peasants who had nothing to do with feudalism, except to support the military and clerical class by their agricultural labour. The village was the normal unit of the peasant population and the agrarian economy, while the administrative unit was the manor, which was under the jurisdiction and economic control of the lord.

These medieval villages were in some ways similar to the late Roman great landed estate or latifundium. In the most Romanised parts of Western Europe, the latter became a medieval village and was described as a villa. There was, however, one important difference between the two. In ancient times agriculture was a venture for profit as long as flourishing cities provided a market for the food, but with the decline in trade and the decline in cities in the early Middle Ages the medieval villa came to produce only enough for its own population and was almost independent of outside sources for its consumption of goods. The village became a self-sufficient economic unit and remained so until the revival of trade and the growth of towns in the twelfth century.

Before the twelfth century at least ninety five percent of the population lived in the country, and the typical economic unit was the village. Villages differed in size and the agricultural pursuits varied from region to region depending on the fertility of soil and natural resources. In a typical village the arable land surrounded a cluster of huts where the peasants lived. The land was generally divided into two open fields, which varied in size from a hundred to more than a thousand acres. The fields were "open", that is, not fenced off into separate plots because husbandry was a cooperative effort. No single peasant was wealthy enough to own a whole team of eight oxen and few even owned a plough. By combining their oxen and ploughs the peasants could cultivate the fields jointly and with greater efficiency than with small plots.

The open fields were divided into strips, the length of which was determined by ploughing with a large team of oxen. The length was usually 200 metres, which was the length oxen could plough without rest, and the width was 5 metres, as a greater width would have required too much effort in turning the team to resume ploughing. The modern acre was derived from the approximate area a medieval team could plow in one day.

The arable land of the village was divided into two fields so the fertility could be preserved by rotation. The field in use was planted about half with autumn sown wheat to be harvested in summer, and half with winter sown wheat to be harvested in autumn. The field that was left fallow was always plowed twice to help it recover its fertility and when not being used provided feed for animals and who provided manure to fertilise the soil.

Under this system the yield was small. Part of the reason for this was that the peasants scattered the seed by hand. Every planting was a race to see if the seeds would germinate before the birds devoured it.

A. Word knowledge: find a word in the text that means the following:

1. land able to be cultivated for the cultivation of crops _____

2. the process or method of varying, in a definite order
   the crops grown on the same ground   _____

3. a great Roman landed estate   _____

4. related to farming   _____

5. a group relating to the production, distribution
   and use of the community property   (2 words)   _____

B. Answer these questions in sentences:

1. Who made up most of the population in the tenth and eleventh century?

   _____

2. What were the Medieval Villages loosely based on?

   _____

3. What were the main differences between the two?

   _____

   _____

   _____

4. Describe a typical village.

   _____

   _____

   _____

5. Why were the fields "open" rather than in individual plots? (Use your own
   words.)

   _____

   _____

6. Why were there two fields?

   _____

7. What was one of the reasons the yield of the fields was small?

   _____

English Poetry Through the Ages: Jacobean and Caroline Poetry

Poetry after the Elizabethan period belonged to one of three strains: the Metaphysical poets, the Cavalier poets and the school of Spencer. However the boundaries between the three groups are not always clear.

The metaphysical poets of the seventeenth century dealt with subjects concerning the abstract in concrete terms. They used logic to explain the inexplicable. The most famous of these is John Donne. Others include George Herbert, Thomas Traherne, Henry Vaughan and Andrew Marvel.

Read the poem by John Donne below.

Death, Be Not Proud

Death be not poud, though some have called thee
Mighty and dreadful, for thou art not so;
For those that thou think'st thou doest overthrow
Die not; poor Death; nor yet canst ye kill me.
From rest and sleep, which but thy picture be,
Much pleasure; then from thee much more must flow;
And soonest with thee our best men doest go—
Rest of their bones and souls' delivery!
Thou'rt slave to fate, chance, kings, and desperate men,
And dost with poison, war and sickness dwell;
And poppy and charms can make us sleep as well
And better than thy stroke. Why swell'st thou then?
One short sleep past, we wake eternally,
And Death shall be no more: Death, thou shalt die!

In this poem Death is told not to be proud since there are other copies of it: rest, sleep, poppies and charms. Donne says those who die enjoy rest for their body and delivery for their soul. It is Death itself that is a slave to death, chance, kings and desperate men. Death is merely a short sleep after which men wake to eternal life.

The poem itself is a simple sonnet. Note the irony in his comments.

Answer these questions:

1. What is the term we use to describe how Death is treated in this poem? Explain this term.

_____

_____

2. Give some of the contrasting examples Donne uses to show Death has no reason to be proud. Why do they work?

_____

_____

3. Donne had strong religious beliefs. What in this poem makes us aware of this?

_____

_____

4. A paradox is a fact which seems to show two opposite ideas at the same time but which needs both ideas to make a truth. Give an example from the poem.

_____

The Cavalier poets wrote in a lighter, more elegant and artificial style than the Metaphysical poets. Poets of this time include Ben Johnson, Richard Lovelace, Robert Herrick, Edmund Waller, Thomas Carew and John Denham. (They were known as Cavaliers because of their loyalty to Charles I during the English Civil War as apposed to the Roundheads.)

Read this poem by Robert Herrick.

To Daffodils

Fair daffodils, we weep to see
You haste away so soon;
As yet the early-rising sun
Has not attain'd his noon.
Stay, stay
Until the hasting day
Has run
But to the evensong;
And, having pray'd together, we
Will go with you along.

We have short time to stay, as you,
We have as short a spring;
As quick a growth to meet decay,
As you, or anything.
We die
As your hours do, and dry
Away
Like to the summer's rain;
Or as the pearls of morning's dew,
Ne'er to be found again.

Answer these questions:

1. What is Herrick saying in the first verse of the poem?

_____

_____

2. Explain how Herrick continues his theme in the second verse of the poem.

_____

_____

3. The theme of this poem may be interpreted several ways. Suggest two possible themes.

_____

_____

4. When Herrick uses the term "as short a spring" what is he referring to?

_____

_____

5. Write the two similes that can be found in verse two. Say what he has used the similes to explain.

_____

_____

Research and Write

The Cavaliers and Roundheads were two opposing sides during the British Civil War. Provide notes that could be used in a debate between the Cavaliers and the Roundheads.

You will need to research the period of Charles I and the differences between the two groups, which were quite wide. You will then need to convert these into simple points that could be used in a debate.

Remember in a debate each person is given only a short time to put forward their view. There are usually three people on each side of the debate and they take one point each. (This does not mean you can just write six short lines.)

You may write your finished notes on page 33.

It would be fun to see if you could find someone to debate one side while you debate the other. Alternatively you could present both sides to your family and ask them to judge which argument was best.

Figures of Speech

Study these definitions and then identify the examples in the questions below and on the next page.

A Simile

In a simile we compare one thing with a generally unlike thing in order to emphasise the quality which it has in common with other things. It generally uses the terms "like" and "as." An example of a simile is "He grunted like a pig.

A Metaphor

A metaphor is a simile taken a step further. It makes a comparison between two unlike things. It states that a thing **is** something other than what it is. For example: I was lost in a sea of nameless faces.

Hyperbole

A hyperbole is an exaggeration aimed at making ones words more effective. The words are not meant to be taken literally: they are figurative.   For example, I am so hungry I could eat an ox.

A Pun

A pun is a play on words, that is, a statement that is made surprising and amusing by using a word that could have two meanings. If it is read with one meaning it is unremarkable, but if read with the other it becomes witty. For example: The roundest knight at King Arthur's table was Sir Circumference. (A circumference is the perimeter of a circle.)

Onomatopeia

Onomatopeia is the name given to language when the words attempt to help the meaning through the sound. Words like cuckoo, buzz, crash, plop are of course onomatopoeia. They directly help the meaning by making the sound of the thing named. The following is by Alexander Pope:

> Soft is the strain when zephyr gently blows,
>
> And smooth stream in smooth numbers flows;
>
> But when loud surges lash the sounding shore,
>
> The hoarse, rough verse should like the torrent roar.

The sound matches and strengthens the sense, in the first couplet of a gentle breeze and in the second couplet of a roaring gale.

Personification: this takes place whenever some object or abstract idea is spoken of as if it were a person. We are apt to personify a ship by referring to it as "she."

1. He finished his work in less than no time. _____

2. He gathered up his belonging and was away like the wind. _____

3. The children were roses in a concrete garden, beautiful and forlorn. _____

4. She had a photographic memory but never developed it. _____

5. Zachery zeroed in on zoo keeping. _____

6. Hark, hark!
Bow-wow.
The watch-dogs bark!
Bow-wow.
Hark, hark! I hear
The straining of strutting chanticleer
Cry, 'cock-a-diddle-dow!"   (William Shaespeare)   _____

7. A horse is a very stable animal. _____

8. Mary arrived at the church with an army of children. _____

9. Carrie's cat clawed her couch, creating chaos. _____

10. The first rays of morning tiptoed through the meadow. _____

11. He's got tons of money. _____

12. He ran as fast as the wind. _____

Similes

A. Similes are common figures of everyday speech. Put each simile below into a sentence. Write a complex sentence and don't just add two or three words.

1. as flat as a pancake: _____

_____

2. as wise as an owl: _____

_____

3. as gentle as a lamb: _____

_____

4. like a tip: _____

_____

B. Explain the following similes.

1. to fight like cats and dogs: _____

2. to sing like an angel: _____

3. to soar like an eagle: _____

Review of Adverbs

An adverb's function is to modify or tell us something more definite about the action of a verb. They may be used to help or modify a verb, an adjective or an adverb.

    For example: I must say he behaved **extraordinarily**. (modify verb)
          John played with an **extraordinarily** heavy racket. (modify adjective)
          We won the match **extraordinarily** easily. (modify adverb)

A. Look at each sentence. State whether the adverb in bold in each sentence modifies a verb, an adjective or an adverb.

1. I am afraid he cheated **slightly**. _____

2. She played **slightly** better this week than last week. _____

3. The young boy **hastily** swallowed an **exceedingly** large lolly. _____

4. She was working **quite happily** on her own. _____

The most common adverbs answer the question how? when? where? They are called **adverbs of manner (how?)** e.g., eagerly, well, expertly; **adverbs of time (when?)** e.g., never, daily, soon, yesterday; **and adverbs of place (where?)** e.g., there, everywhere.

Underline the adverb and state whether it is an adverb of manner, time or place.

1. My friend arrived punctually at six o'clock. _____

2. The hunter prematurely pulled the trigger and missed the rabbit.

    _____

3. He was not living there at the time. _____

4. He was working hard then but now he is on holiday.

    _____

5. I can see perfectly well here. _____

6. He rarely visits me. _____

7. He emphatically denied the accusations. _____

8. The damage to the water supply must be repaired immediately.

    _____

Word Forms

Rewrite the following sentences changing the underlined words to the correct form.

1. The kitten played **mischievous** with the wool.

   _____

2. The officer pointed out the **direct** I was to head in.

   _____

3. He is **reputation** to be something of a genius at maths.

   _____

4. One can only say that the diplomats were treated **deplorable**.

   _____

5. With great **anticipated** the crowd watched as the gymnast began her routine.

   _____

6. The **hostility** audience booed the performance.

   _____

7. The judge expressed some **cynical** at the hardened criminal's repentance.

   _____

8. The young golfer spoke **sarcasm** to his caddy.

   _____

9. The air–raffic controller **perspiration** freely as she noticed the plane's deviation from course.

   _____

   _____

10. A **carelessness** approach to marriage has often been identified as an important cause of **separate**.

   _____

   _____

11. As the crowd watched, the athlete fell, groaning in **agony** pain.

   _____

The Medieval Village

Most villages had certain common features. These included a meadow from which sufficient hay could be mowed to feed the oxen during winter, but this source of food was not always adequate and frequently animals had to be killed, making it hard for the village to increase the number of oxen.

If larger pastures were available then herds of cattle and flocks of sheep were kept to provide milk, cheese and wool. Woodland was also important as the main source of fuel and building material. Other assets common to most villages were a pond or stream, from which fish were caught, a mill for grinding corn and a common oven for baking bread. Roads and paths led to and from the village.

Most villages had a church or chapel, which was an important part of their life. The church was endowed, for the use of the priest, with a holding or Glebe consisting of strips scattered through the open fields and a share in the meadow pastures and woods, just like the other peasant tenants. Although the parson was free, he usually participated in the husbandry of the village and was himself a peasant. Those higher in the bureaucracy of the church, for example bishops, had their own manor and serfs to work for them.

A village of any size or consequence would also have a substantial house for the lord, which was set apart from the peasants hut. This house was originally called the manor. Since the village was thought of as belonging to the lord's residence, and was under the jurisdiction of the court he held in his hall, the term was later extended to include the whole village over which the lord had proprietary and jurisdictional rights. It then became usual to refer to the lord's house as the manor-house or hall and the village as his manor.

The manorial organisation of medieval villages was a result of the slow evolution and combination from both the Roman villa and the Germanic village community. The essence of the manor was the subordination of peasantry to the lord of the manor. The slavery of Roman times disappeared and resembled the late Roman estates where the peasants were free but tied to the land. In Germanic communities the local chief's political power was recognised by the village and he received customary gifts, from them. The agricultural life of the Germanic village was communal. After the fifth century the free men of the village became dependent peasants tied to the soil and subject to the authority of the local lord. who protected them in return for economic support.

By the ninth century the legal notions of both the Roman and Germanic tribes had been assimilated in a greater or lesser degree from region to region, until the manor became the typical unit of economic administration. Then with the disintegration of the central government in the ninth and tenth centuries the economic control of the lord was enhanced by the addition of the local jurisdiction, or political authority, exercised over the peasants of his manor, so that by the eleventh century every lord of the manor had his court. Thus the manorial court became the heart and core of every manor.

A. Word knowledge: find a word in the text that means the following:

1. the range or area of legal or other authority _____

2. provided with a lasting source of income _____

3. taken in and included as part of one's own _____

4. belonging to or controlled as property _____

5. the lesser or secondary importance of _____

B. Answer these questions:

1. List the common features found in most villages.

_____

_____

_____

2. What was a Glebe?

_____

_____

3. In a simple sentence explain what the lord had control over.

_____

4. Think. Under the feudal system, why do you think the manorial court became so important?

_____

_____

_____

5. Why do you think villages had communal ovens?

_____

C. Grammar

1. Identify and write below every adverb in the first paragraph on page 38.

_____

2. Identify and write below every adjective in the first paragraph on page 38.

_____

English Poetry Through the Ages: The Restoration and the 18th Century Poets

Oliver Cromwell ruled England under a Protectorate until his death. Following this a series of battles ensued and Charles II was restored to the throne in 1661. A world of fashion and scepticism emerged and this encouraged poets to write satires as well. A satire is a literary work that uses irony, sarcasm and ridicule to show up something silly or evil by representing it in a laughable way.

The major poets of this period were Samuel Butler, John Dryden, Alexander Pope, Samuel Johnson and Jonathon Swift. These poets all had admiration for the ancient world and aimed for a polished style in emulation of the Romans. Dryden translated all the known works of Virgil and Pope produced versions of two Homeric epics.

Below you will find a few lines from "Hudibras" by Samuel Butler. Hudibras is a mock-heroic narrative poem commenting satirically on the Roundheads, Puritans, Presbyterians and many of the other factions in the civil war. The epic tells the story of Sir Hudibras a knight. Read it carefully.

> Sir Hudibras his passing worth,
> The manner how he sallied forth;
> His arms and equipage are shown;
> His horse's virtues, and his own.
> Th' adventure of the bear and fiddle
> Is sung, but breaks off in the middle.
> When civil dudgeon first grew high,
> And men fell out they knew not why;
> When hard words, jealousies and fears
> Set folks together by the ears,
> And made them fight, like mad or drunk,
> For Dame Religion as for punk;
> Whose honesty they all dare swear for,
> Though not a man of them knew wherefore:
> With long-ear'd route, to battle sounded,
> And pulpit, drum ecclesiastick,
> Was beat with fist, instead of stick;
> Then did Sir Knight abandon dwelling.
> And out he rode a colonelling.

This poem is written in iambic tetrameter in closed couplets. Closed couplets are two lines of verse that do not extend their sense beyond the line's end.

Since this poem was published only four years after Charles II was restored to the throne the poem found an appreciative audience.

A. Answer these questions:

1. Look at the poem above. Give an example of a closed couplet.

   _____

   _____

2. Do you think Sir Hudibras in the first four lines is described satirically or literally? Explain why.

   _____

   _____

3. Why do you think this poem was very popular?

   _____

The poem that follows is an extract from "Autumn" by Samuel Johnson. It is a totally different type of poem to the previous one. His works, both in poetry and literature were extensive during this period.

> Alas! with swift and silent pace,
> Impatient time rolls on the year;
> The Seasons change, and Nature's face
> Now sweetly smiles, now frowns severe.
>
> 'Twas Spring, 'twas Summer, all was gay,
> Now Autumn bends a cloudy brow;
> The flowers of Spring are swept away,
> And Summer fruits desert the bough.
>
> The verdant leaves that play'd on high,
> And wanton'd on the western breeze,
> Now trod in dust neglected lie,
> As Boreas strips the bending trees.
>
> The fields that waved with golden grain,
> As russet heaths are wild and bare;
> Not moist with dew, but drench'd in rain,
> Nor health nor pleasure wanders there.

B. Answer these questions:

1. What is personified in the poem?

   _____

2. Give examples of the personification.

_____

_____

3. How does personifying Nature add depth to the poem?

_____

_____

4. Complete: The couplets rhyme in _____.

The extract below is taken from an epic poem by Alexander Pope, "Essay on Man." It is a rationalistic effort to use philosophy in order to "vindicate the ways of God to man." It is concerned with the natural order God has decreed for man. It claims that as man can not know God's purpose he can not complain about his purpose in the great chain of events. Read it carefully as it is very skilfully written.

Know then thyself, presume not God to scan,
The proper study of mankind is man.
Placed on this isthmus of a middle state,
A being darkly wise, and rudely great:
With too much knowledge for the sceptic side,
With too much weakness for the stoic's pride,
He hangs between; in doubt to act or rest;
In doubt to deem himself a God or beast;
In doubt his mind or body to prefer;
Born but to die, and reasoning but to err;
Alike in ignorance, his reasoning such,
Whether he thinks too little or too much:
Chaos of thought and passion, all confused;
Still by himself abused or disabused;
Created half to rise and half to fall;
Great lord of all things, yet prey to all;
Sole judge of truth, in endless error hurled:
The glory, jest and riddle of the world.

Think then answer these questions;

1. Give examples of the way Pope has skilfully used words to emphasise his views.

_____

_____

2. Explain the meaning of the terms you have chosen.

_____

_____

3. Summarise in your own words what Pope is saying in his poem.

_____

_____

_____

_____

Although the microscope had not yet been invented there was a growing belief in the scientific community that there were smaller components in everything which we could not be seen. This poem by Margaret Cavendish is for your enjoyment.

A World Made by Atomes

Small atomes of themselves a World may make,
As being subtle, and of every shape:
And as they dance about, fit places finde,
Such Formes as best agree, make every kinde.
For when we build a house of Bricke, and Stone,
We lay them even, every one by one:
And when we finde a gap that's big, or small,
We seeke out Stones, to fit that place withall.
For when not fit, too big, or little be,
They fall away, and cannot stay we see.
So Atomes, as they dance, finde places fit,
They there remaine, lye close, and fast will sticke.
Those that unfit, the rest that rove about,
Do never leave, untill they thrust them out.
Thus by their severall Motions, and their Formes,
As severall work-men serve each others turnes.
And thus, by chance, may a New World create:
Or else predestined to worke my Fate.

Research and Write:

Research and write a biography of the life of any of the poets whose poetry you have explored since page 40. (Samuel Butler, Samuel Johnson, Alexander Pope or Margaret Cavendish.) Follow all of the rules for writing a biography you have been taught in previous English books.

More French Words and Phrases Used in English

Match the definition to the correct word or phrase in the box. Learn what you do not know.

café au lait, maître d', faux pas, protégé, par excellence, attache haute coutre, piece de resistance, en route, cordon bleu, au fait, en suite, hors d'oeuvre, potpourri, petit four, matinee, déjà vu,

1. a feeling like you have that you have already seen or done something when you are sure you haven't _____

2. on the way _____

3. small desert, especially a cake _____

4. high class, expensive clothing styles _____

5. the day's first showing of a movie or play _____

6. someone whose training is sponsored by an influential person _____

7. an appetizer before the main meal _____

8. master of the dining room _____

9. preeminent, the best of the best _____

10. conversant with, informed _____

11. a scented mixture of dried flowers and spices; a miscellaneous group or collection _____

12. part of a set, together, often used to refer to a small bathroom joined onto a bedroom _____

13. an outstanding accomplishment or the final part of something e.g., a project, meal etc. _____

14. person assigned to a diplomatic post _____

15. coffee with milk _____

16. "blue ribbon" in cookery, Master Chef _____

17. a foolish mistake, something that shouldn't be done _____

Common Figurative Expressions

Choose a figurative expression from the box at the bottom to fit each meaning. Write it on the line. If you do not know them, learn them.

1. a subject that causes keen and general discussion _____

2. to call attention to one's own good qualities _____

3. not to seek revenge for an injury _____

4. to waste time adding to something of which there is already ample _____

5. to like being seen, heard and noticed by the public _____

6. to avoid being friendly with someone _____

7. to extract and make use of another's ideas _____

8. to give someone the information necessary to understand what is happening _____

9. to cause people to quarrel _____

10. that reminds me of something I have heard before _____

11. a subject that leads to bitter argument _____

12. close together, side by side _____

13. an unwanted person causing trouble in the group _____

14. a reserve method of action in case the first fails _____

to carry coals to Newcastle	to put someone in the picture
a burning question	to set people by the ears
to keep someone at arm's length	that rings a bell
to blow one's own trumpet	cheek by jowl
a bone of a contention	a second string to one's bow
to like being in the limelight	to pick someone's brain
to turn the other cheek	a cuckoo in the nest

© Valerie Marett
Coroneos Publications

Australian Homeschooling #562
Successful English 8A

Review of Pronouns

There are nine main classes of pronouns:

- **Personal:** these are the most common pronouns. The first person pronouns are: **I, me, we, us.** The second person is: <u>you</u>. The third person are: he, him, she, her, it, they, them.

- **Impersonal:** the pronoun **it** when it does not refer to any person or thing, e.g., It is raining.

- **Relative:** these are the words **who, whom, whose, which, that** when they are used to join one clause to another, e.g., He was reading the book which I lent him.

- **Interrogative:** **who, whoever, whose, which, what, whatever** are interrogative when they introduce questions, e.g., Who is at the door?

- **Reflexive:** The words **myself, himself, herself, yourself, itself, ourselves, your-selves, themselves** are all reflective pronouns because they reflect the action back on the doer, e.g., The girl cut herself with the knife.

- **Possessive:** These pronouns denote possession: **mine, his, hers, its, ours, yours, theirs,** e.g., This pen is his. The word "his" stands in place of "his pen."

- **Distributive:** The words **either, neither, each** are singular distributive pronouns, e.g., The boys wanted to go, but neither of them was able to.

- **Demonstrative:** the demonstrative pronoun this, that, these, those stand in-stead of a demonstrative adjective and its noun, e.g., "I will buy this," said the shopper, "but I don't want that." (This might stand for a cake.)

- **Indefinite:** Such words as **one, anyone, anybody, anything, someone, some-thing, no-one, nobody, none, any all, some, nothing, everything, everyone, everybody** all stand instead of an indefinite noun, e.g., Some like everything and some like nothing.

On the line write the pronoun or pronouns in each sentence and state what type of pronoun it is.

1. "Between you and me, John, I think your idea of climate change is crazy," said Robert, scratching himself behind his ear, which seemed to be irritating him.
   "What do you mean?" asked Robert. "Someone had to scientifically research it."

   _____

   _____

2. Hand me that hammer, please, Mary. _____

3. I can see myself in the mirror. _____

4. Neither of us believed a word Michael said. _____

5. What do you want me to do about the mail
while you are away? _____

6. That is incredible. _____

7. Students who cheat in a test are only
hurting themselves. _____

8. Several of these slices of bread are mouldy. _____

9. Each new day is different. _____

10. Somebody has let the cat inside. _____

11. It is dangerous to play with fire. _____

12. She married someone whom I really admire. _____

13. This book is hers and that book is mine. _____

14. They have each been told about the accident. _____

Word Knowledge

Write a single word for each of the following:

1. The sum of words that a person knows and can use _____

2. A drama with an unhappy ending _____

3. An exchange of ideas or opinions between two
or more people _____

4. Belonging to common or familiar speech _____

5. A brief account that omits details _____

6. A sharing in feelings of another _____

7. Agreed to by everyone _____

The Lord of the Manor's Rights

The lord of the Manor had both economic and political rights. The demesne of the lord of the manor was from one quarter to one third of the arable land. This land was not occupied by peasants but was reserved for the lord and made productive by the peasants' labour. It was intermixed with the peasants' tenements and scattered like theirs throughout the two or three fields.

The basic obligation of the peasant was to plough, plant and harvest the demesne of the lord, and the ordinary peasant fulfilled this duty by what was called "week-work" and "boon work." During most of the year he devoted three days a week to cultivating the demesne and during the harvest season gave all his labour to the demesne before harvesting his own crop.

On many manors there were peasants who were free men although they held tenements within the manor. From these, lighter labour on the demesne was required and in some cases no labour was required. Some peasants possessed smaller tenements than those of ordinary peasants and were of lower social status. Only the free peasants had any legal rights against the lord of the manor and it seems that custom prevented the lord from subjecting the peasants to more than the usual services.

Parts of the meadow was in the demesne, but this usually consisted of a certain percentage of the hay produced and the equivalent proportion of the grazing rights after the haymaking was finished. These rights were measured in the number of the lord's animals allowed to graze. In the same way the demesne also extended over the pasture, the woodlands, the waste, the stream or pond, and other so-called "appurtenances" of the manor like the mill, the oven and the roads. The demesne right varied from a proportionate share to full ownership subject to the customary use of the peasants. In return for such customary use peasants owed, according to their personal status or according to the various size of their tenements certain services or payments to the lord.

The various payments constituted a substantial part of his manorial revenue. The most important of these were the "heriot", a customary fee exacted by the lord on the death of a peasant and "merchet", which was payment for permission for the daughter of a peasant to marry a man who was not the lord's peasant. These two payments were only levied on those peasants who were not free. However the "tallage" or "taille" was levied on all peasants and was an arbitrary tax the lord of the manor could exact at will and in any amount, although it was usually levied at regular intervals, and in proportion to the peasant's tenement.

The lord of the manor was a vassal and spent much time serving his feudal lord or else hunting or amusing himself in other ways. Kings, dukes, margraves and counts had little time for manorial duties and entrusted them to officials representatives. In later manorial times the representative was known as the baliff or steward. He was assisted by subordinate officials chosen from the peasants called provosts or reeves, who supervised the peasants' activities.

The lord enforced his jurisdiction over the peasants by his military might, which could be brought against them if need be. However most ordinary disputes were settled in the court of the manor by the baliff using rules laid down from generation to generation within the village community.

A. Find a word in the text that means the following:

1. the overseer of the manor appointed by the lord _____

2. all the land that was retained by the lord of the manor for his own use _____

3. collective name for the right to use the mill, the oven and the roads _____

4. tax extracted on the death of a peasant _____

5. three days during each week, for most of the year, that the peasant devoted to cultivating the lord's land _____

6. an arbitrary tax the lord could levy at will on all peasants _____

7. peasant chosen by baliff to supervise the peasants activities _____

8. payment for permission for a peasant's daughter to marry another lord's peasant _____

B. Answer these questions:

1. How much of the area surrounding the manor was the lord's demesne?

_____

2. Did all peasants have equal amount of land or equal rights? Explain your answer.

_____

_____

3. What was the lord's manorial revenue made up of? Don't miss anything.

_____

_____

4. What did the peasants welfare depend on? Explain fully. You may use a separate piece of paper to write your answer on.

English Poetry Through the Ages: The Romantic Movement

The last quarter of the 18th century was a time of social and political turbulence in the U.S., France, Ireland and elsewhere. In England movement for change and more inclusive power sharing was growing and from this the Romantic movement in English poetry developed.

The main poets of this period were William Blake, William Wordsworth, Samuel Taylor Coleridge, Percy Bysshe Shelley, Lord Byron and John Keats.

This period emphasised the creative expression of the individual and the need to find and formulate new forms of expression. To the Romantics the moment of creation was the most important in poetic expression and could not be repeated. They also made a shift in language to express the language of the common man so more were able to enjoy it.

The poem below is written by William Blake and is probably his best known poem. It was even put to music in 1916. During this period there had been an industrial revolution. Wool and cotton mills had been built and and people, many of them children, worked in them in appalling conditions. During the same period a religious reformation took place in England and out of it arose many of the great reformists like Lord Shaftesbury, John Howard, Elizabeth Fry.

Blake acknowledged the state of society and suggested that it was depraved and corrupt. He wondered how a Christian country could allow this to happen and vowed that he would not cease to fight until things had changed.

Read the poem.

Jerusalem

And did those feet in ancient time
Walk upon England's mountains green?
And was the holy Lamb of God
On England's pleasant pastures seen?

And did the Countenance Divine
Shine forth upon our clouded hills?
And was Jerusalem builded here
Among these dark satanic mills?

Bring me my bow of burning gold!
Bring me my arrows of desire!
Bring me my spear! O clouds, unfold!
Bring me my chariot of fire!

I will not cease from mental fight,
Nor shall my sword sleep in my hand,
Till we have built Jerusalem
In England's green and pleasant land.

Answer these questions:

1. It has been suggested that England and Jerusalem have been used as metaphors. What do you think they represent?

   _____

   _____

2. The first two verses pose questions. Give an example of one of these questions and explain it.

   _____

   _____

3. The third verse contains vivid imagery. What does this imagery suggest?

   _____

   _____

4. The last verse suggests a mental fight. Was this mental fight with himself or with others? What form will the fight take?

   _____

   _____

Another poet of this time was William Wordsworth. His most famous poem is shown below. Read it.

The Daffodil
I wandered lonely as a cloud
That floats on high o'er vales and hills,
When all at once I saw a crowd,
A host, of golden daffodils;
Beside the lake, beneath the trees,
Fluttering and dancing in the breeze.

Continuous as the stars that shine
And twinkle on the milky way,
They stretched in never-ending line
Along the margin of a bay:
Ten thousand saw I at a glance,
Tossing their heads in sprightly dance.

The waves beside them danced; but they
Out-did the sparkling waves in glee:
A poet could not but be gay,
In such a jocund company:
I gazed---and gazed---but little thought
What wealth the show to me had brought:

For oft, when on my couch I lie
In vacant or in pensive mood,
They flash upon that inward eye
Which is the bliss of solitude;
And then my heart with pleasure fills,
And dances with the daffodils.

Answer these questions:

1. Summarise what the poet is saying in this poem.

_____

_____

_____

_____

2. The poem is full of vivid similes. Give two examples.

_____

_____

3. Personification occurs in the first verse. Explain what it is.

_____

_____

4. The poem is in rhyming couplets. Give an example.

_____

Research and Write:

Write an essay outlining the cause and effect of the Industrial Revolution in England.

- Briefly explain the system before the Industrial Revolution

- Outline how it occurred and its long term benefits and effects.

- Finish with your conclusions.

Inserting Proper Nouns

Insert the proper noun from the box into the correct space below.

Sarah-Anne, Titanic, Edison, Nelson, Italian, New Guinea, Auckland, Easter, Nile, igneous, Beethoven, Columbus, Queen Elizabeth, Tasmania, England, Everest, QANTAS, Atlantic, Mercury, Ford, Asia, March,

1. country _____

2. month _____

3. city _____

4. ocean _____

5. inventor _____

6. airline _____

7. planet _____

8. explorer _____

9. admiral _____

10. car _____

11. ship _____

12. river _____

13. island _____

14. composer _____

15. mountain _____

16. language _____

17. holiday _____

18. title _____

19. state _____

20. girl _____

21. rock _____

22. continent _____

Food Twins

Complete the following by matching the food with a word from the box.

beans, tomato sauce, spaghetti, jelly, marmalade, chips, butter, mint sauce, apples, crackers, eggs, cream

1. oranges and _____

2. bacon and _____

3. fish and _____

4. bread and _____

5. apple pie and _____

6. meat pie and _____

6. lamb and _____

8. ice cream and _____

9. cheese and _____

10. pork and _____

11. meatballs and _____

12. toast and _____

Word Knowledge

Complete each sentence below using a word from the box. Before you start use a dictionary to look up any word you are not sure of.

> cudgelling, acclimatised, infantile, pusillanimous, matricide, evasive, adjourn, insular, monogram, buoyant, mitigating, recriminations, allegation, despicable

1. "We have not finished," said the chairman, "but it is getting very late; we had better _____ our meeting.

2. As there was no _____ circumstances, the judge had no option but to sentence him to the maximum term of imprisonment.

3. The adjective to ribe anyone whom you consider to be lacking in courage and general strength of mind is _____.

4. The artist designed him a _____ from his initials.

5. The shopkeeper said he had been hit over the head but the thief denied the _____.

6. A person who won't give a straight answer is said to be _____.

7. By murdering his mother, Nero was guilty of _____.

8. We say a person is in a _____ mood when he feels light-hearted.

9. At first we found the tropical heat overpowering, but we soon became _____.

10. Their hurled accusations at each other until the room rang with their _____.

11. My homework was puzzling me, when my father came by and asked "What are you _____ your brains about?"

12. Those who lie to secure an advantage are _____ creatures.

13. His views were very _____ as they had never been broadened by travel.

14. "Don't be so _____, John," Dad said. "You are not a baby."

Filling Out A Form

Whenever someone enters a country they are asked to fill out and sign a form. This form is a legal document. Penalties apply for making a false statement. Read the form below carefully and fill it out. Assume you have been on holiday and may be bringing back souvenirs.

Family Surname: _____   Given Name: _____

Passport Number: _____

Name of ship or Flight No: _____

Intended address in Australia: _____

_____

Do you intend to live in Australia for the next 12 months?   Yes/No   ☐   ☐

If you are not an Australian citizen:

Do you have tuberculosis?   Yes   ☐   No   ☐

Do you have any criminal conviction/s   Yes   ☐   No   ☐

<u>You must answer every question</u> —if unsure   Yes   ☒

Are you bringing into Australia:

1. Goods that may be prohibited or subject to restrictions, such as medicines, steroids, illegal pornography, fire arms, weapons or illicit drugs?   Yes   No   ☐   ☐

2. More than 2250 ml of alcohol or 250 cigarettes or 250gm tobacco?   Yes   No   ☐   ☐

3. Goods obtained overseas or purchased duty and/or tax free in Australia with a combined total price of more than AUD$900, including gifts?   Yes   No   ☐   ☐

4. Goods/samples for business/commercial use?   Yes   No   ☐   ☐

5. AUD$10,000 or more in Australian or foreign currency?
   Note: if a customs or police officer asks, you must report travellers cheques, cheques, money orders or other bearer negotiable instruments of any amount.   Yes   No   ☐   ☐

6. Any food—includes dried, fresh, preserved, cooked or uncooked?   Yes   No   ☐   ☐

7. Wooden articles, plants, parts of plants, traditional medicines or herbs, seeds, bulbs, straw, nuts?   Yes   No   ☐   ☐

8. Animals, parts of animals, animal products including equipment, pet food, eggs, biological, specimens, birds, fish, insects, shells, bee products?   Yes   No   ☐   ☐

9. Soil, items with soil attached or used in fresh water areas i.e. sports/recreational equipment, shoes?   Yes   No   ☐   ☐

10. Were you in Africa, South/Central America or the Caribbean in the last 6 days?   Yes   No   ☐   ☐

Declaration: The information I have given is true, correct and complete. I understand failure to answer any question may have serious consequences.

Signature: _____   Date:_____

Australian Homeschooling #562
Successful English 8A

Review of Prepositions

A preposition introduces a phrase. It stands before a noun or its equivalent. We say it governs a noun. It also shows relationship between a noun and another word.

For example: We walked along the wall. The preposition along governs the word wall and introduces the adverbial phrase. It shows the relationship between walked and wall.

A. Look at each sentence below. Study each underlined preposition. State:
- **what noun or noun equivalent it governs**
- **what phrase it introduces**
- **between what two words it shows the relationship.**

1. We ran **across** the paddock at top speed.

   _____

2. People used to believe **in** the man **in** the moon.

   _____

   _____

3. The boy **with** the black eye looked very sad.

   _____

B. Complete each phrase below with one of the following prepositions: between, beneath, for, from, within, behind.

1. _____ range

2. _____ the duration

3. _____ bad to worse

4. _____ contempt

5. _____ one's back

6. _____ two stools

C. Choose the correct phrase from the box to fit each meaning and underline the preposition.

within a stone's throw; without counting the cost;
under a cloud; between two fires; up to the hilt:

1. to the fullest extent   _____

2. exposed to danger on both sides   _____

3. quite near   _____

4. involved completely in something _____

5. suspected of doing something wrong _____

Some verbs take different prepositions according to their use.

For example we say:

account **for** a thing	but	account **to** a person
agree **to** something	but	agree **with** someone
appeal **to** a person or court	but	appeal **against** a decision
argue **with** a person	but	argue **for** or **against** a proposal
confer **with** someone	but	confer **about** something
correspond **with** someone	but	correspond (resemble) **to** something
		about something
divide **between** two	but	divide **among** many
entrust a person **with** a thing	but	entrust a thing **to** a person
exchange a thing **with** a person	but	exchange a thing **for** something else
impress something **on** a person	but	impress someone **with** something
inquire **of** the person asked	but	inquire **after** or **about** the object of an inquiry
intrude **on** a person	but	intrude **into** a matter that does not concern you
invest money **in** something	but	invest someone **with** an honour
part **from** someone	but	part **with** something
result **from** a cause	but	result **in** an effect

Insert the correct preposition in the following sentences.

1. I have impressed _____ him the need to hurry.

2. He conferred _____ his salesman _____ the drive for bigger sales.

3. Many accidents result _____ pure carelessness.

4. Take these lollies and divide them equally _____ the six children.

5. The wing of a bird corresponds _____ the arm of a man.

6. Having inquired _____ his wife, who had been ill, I parted _____ him at the bus stop.

7. It is useless to argue _____ him _____ his decision; he is adamant.

8. I had to account _____ the manager _____ the loss of the stock.

9. I have entrusted Jim _____ the money to give to Mr Clark.

10. It is wise not to intrude _____ matters of business that do not concern you.

11. I shall appeal _____ the courts _____ this unfair decision.

The Fall and Rise of Towns

During the barbarian invasions the military towns on the frontiers increased in number, and both on the border, and the towns throughout the Empire, the main object of the town was as a means of defence or a place to attack from. Thus towns suffered greatly during the barbarian invasions. When the storm had passed many of the towns lay in ruins. Rome itself was sacked many times, while in Britain a considerable part of the Roman towns seemed to have been wiped out by the Anglo-Saxon invaders. It was not just the violence of the destroyers of the Empire that brought so many cities to ruin. What chiefly caused their depopulation and ruin was the preference of the barbarians for the open country and a dislike of life within city walls. It was therefore inevitable that city life would give place to country life.

As the invaders settled down and civilization began to revive, the old Roman towns began to assume something of their old importance and new towns began to spring up in areas where the towns had been swept away. Then came the invasion of the Vikings, Magyars and Saracens, and, with no strong central government, the larger towns were thrown upon their own resources for defence. They armed themselves with fighting men, and surrounded themselves with strong, high walls and so Europe became full of strong-walled towns, the counterpart of the castles of the feudal lords, which were the defence of the countryside.

These towns, scattered over every feudal state, were vassals of the feudal overlord, owed allegiance to him, had to pay him feudal dues and aid in his war enterprises. At first each householder in the town was a tenant of the lord of the fief and was individually responsible for the services due to the lord. It was not until the towns came to act in the corporate capacity that they became an important part of the political system.

In the ninth century society was divided into three classes: the clergy; the feudal nobles; and the peasantry. Before long a fourth class emerged, the bourgeoisie or middle class, who dwelt in the towns and who were dependent on commerce. This had gradually declined since the Germanic invasions in western Europe. The Mediterranean routes were gradually dominated by the Saracens although the Byzantine navy kept the sea route open for trade with Venice. In the north the Vikings had destroyed any trade routes that were there. Trade did not cease completely, but it became unimportant. Local markets were held and hawkers peddled wares from village to village.

However, in the eleventh century trade began to revive, due largely to the growth in local population, since agricultural production had not kept pace with that growth. The earliest revival of trade in the west resulted from the sale at high prices in famine stricken areas of basic necessities, such as grain and cattle, bought at low prices in plentiful regions. Economic revival resulted in the reopening of the Mediterranean routes to the East, but it was necessary to increase wealth in the West before luxuries were sold to the East.

Australian Homeschooling #562
Successful English 8A

Answer these questions:

1. Why would the towns have mainly been used as places of defence or of means to attack from?

   _____

   _____

   _____

2. What was the chief cause of the decline of the towns after the barbarian invasions?

   _____

   _____

3. Towns revived but then there was an invasion of Vikings, Magyars and Saracens. What did this force the larger towns to do?

   _____

   _____

4. List the duties the towns owed their feudal lord as his vassal.

   _____

   _____

5. In the ninth century what were the three classes?

   _____

   _____

6. What fourth class emerged?

   _____

7. Would the size of towns be more dependent on local agriculture or on trade? Explain your answer.

   _____

   _____

B. Word knowledge: find a word in the text that means the following:

1. group of people who acted together   _____

2. holding a function that is similar to   _____

3. middle-class   _____

English Poetry Through the Ages:
The Romantic Movement 2

Samuel Taylor Coleridge was a poet, literary critic and friend of William Wordsworth. Kubla Khan is one of his most famous and enduring poems. Colridge claims that he was reading the story of Kubla Khan, in which he commanded the building of a new palace, and fell asleep. While he slept he dreamed of it and awoke to write a poem.

Kubla Khan ordered the pleasure palace to be built near the sacred river Alph. Walls and towers were raised around it with beautiful gardens and woods. The river ran through the woods finally running into the sea.

In the last verse he speaks of once having seen an Abyssian maid who played sweetly and says if he could he would rebuild the pleasure dome out of her music.

Read the extract below taken from the poem:

> In Xanadu did Kubla Khan
> A stately pleasure dome decree:
> Where Alph, the sacred river, ran
> Through caverns measureless to man
> Down to a sunless sea.
> So twice five miles of fertile ground
> With walls and towers were girdled round:
> And there were gardens bright with sinuous rills,
> Where blossomed many an incense-bearing tree;
> And here were forests ancient as the hills,
> Enfolding sunny spots of greenery.
>
> But oh! that deep romantic chasm which slanted
> Down the green hill athwart a cedarn cover!
> A savage place! as holy and enchanted
> As e'er beneath a waning moon was haunted
> By woman wailing for her demon lover!
> And from this chasm, with ceaseless turmoil seething,
> As if this earth in fast thick pants were breathing,
> A mighty fountain momently was forced:
> Amid whose swift half-intermitted burst
> Huge fragments vaulted like rebounding hail,
> Or chaffy grain beneath the thresher's flail:
> And 'mid these dancing rocks at once and ever
> It flung up momently the sacred river.
> Five miles meandering with a mazy motion
> Through wood and dale the sacred river ran,
> Then reached the caverns measureless to man,

And sank in tumult to a lifeless ocean:
And 'mid this tumult Kubla heard from far
Ancestral voices prophesying war!

Note the musical incantation of the poem.

Answer these questions:

1. The poem rhymes in _____ lines. Give examples of these rhymes.

2. Do the last two lines provide a contrast to the rest of the poem? Explain your answer.

   _____

   _____

   _____

3. Find other contrasts within the poem.

   _____

   _____

The following poem by Percy Bysse Shelley also has a historical theme. In this poem, the speaker learns from a traveller about a giant ruined statue of King Ramses II of Egypt.

Read the poem carefully and notice the mocking contrast at the end.

Ozymandias

I met a traveller from an antique land
Who said: `Two vast and trunkless legs of stone
Stand in the desert. Near them, on the sand,
Half sunk, a shattered visage lies, whose frown,
And wrinkled lip, and sneer of cold command,
Tell that its sculptor well those passions read
Which yet survive, stamped on these lifeless things,
The hand that mocked them and the heart that fed.
And on the pedestal these words appear --
"My name is Ozymandias, king of kings:
Look on my works, ye Mighty, and despair!"
Nothing beside remains. Round the decay
Of that colossal wreck, boundless and bare
The lone and level sands stretch far away.'

Answer these questions:

1. What do you think is the theme of the poem?

_____

_____

2. Explain how the poet has written the poem in such a way as to mock the statement by Ramses "My name is Ozymandias, king of kings: Look on my works, ye Mighty, and despair!"

_____

_____

3. Give at least three examples of the clever use of imagery by the author to provide a vivid image.

_____

_____

Note the difference in the style of writing of Coleridge and Shelley.

John Keats was one of the major poets of the Romantic Movement although his work was only published four years before his death and it was only after his death that his reputation grew. He has become one of the most beloved of English poets.

The poem below, "A Thing of Beauty", beauty and its nature mesmerises us and takes away any sorrow we feel from time to time. Read the poem below:

A Thing of Beauty

A thing of beauty is a joy for ever:
Its lovliness increases; it will never
Pass into nothingness; but still will keep
A bower quiet for us, and a sleep
Full of sweet dreams, and health, and quiet breathing.
Therefore, on every morrow, are we wreathing
A flowery band to bind us to the earth,
Spite of despondence, of the inhuman dearth
Of noble natures, of the gloomy days,
Of all the unhealthy and o'er-darkn'd ways
Made for our searching: yes, in spite of all,
Some shape of beauty moves away the pall
From our dark spirits. Such the sun, the moon,
Trees old and young, sprouting a shady boon
For simple sheep; and such are daffodils

With the green world they live in; and clear rills
That for themselves a cooling covert make
'Gainst the hot season; the mid-forest brake,
Rich with a sprinkling of fair musk-rose blooms:
And such too is the grandeur of the dooms
We have imagined for the mighty dead;
An endless fountain of immortal drink,
Pouring unto us from the heaven's brink.

Answer these questions:

1. What examples does Keats give of beauty?

   _____

   _____

2. "Simple sheep" is a metaphor. Of what is Keats speaking when he uses it?

   _____

3. What effect does the poet say these beautiful things have upon us?

   _____

   _____

Research and write:

Write an information report of at least 500 words on the Mongol, Kublai Khan.

Include:

- background details about the Mongols, who they were and their rise.
- Kublai Khan's lineage
- describe his rise to power.
- outline his achievements
- the influence of the Chinese culture on him
- describe any problems that occurred during his reign
- did his dynasty continue after his death? If not, why not?

Make sure you write a rough copy and correct it before attaching a good copy.

Removing Ambiguity

It is important to write correctly so there is no ambiguity. Ambiguity is doubt or uncertainty regarding what the writer intended in either words, pictures or other media. Text speak is an excellent example of ambiguity.

Rewrite the following sentences so the meaning becomes clear.

1. The lawyer harangued the jury from a distant town.

   _____

2. For Sale: a house for $100,000. It won't last long so see us now.

   _____

3. I like Luna Park more than my girlfriend.

   _____

4. For the experience of a lifetime drink GoGo energy drink. You'll never get better.

   _____

   _____

5. When the car hit the truck the truck's load shifted and pinned the lower half of the driver's body. This had to be removed to free him.

   _____

   _____

6. Being something of a wreck, the buyer was able to get a special deal on the car.

   _____

7. The boy emerged from the house with a very odd look.

   _____

8. Mashed or not mashed, Australians like potatoes.

   _____

9. He took the bull home well pleased with the day's work.

   _____

10. The jug hit him on the head which was fortunately empty.

   _____

Knowledge of Nouns

Look up these words in a dictionary and then complete the exercises below.

inspection	preface	directory	courier	quiver
scabbard	inventory	prologue	inquest	phial
haulier	experiment	preamble	catalogue	

1. Choose from the list a noun that means a list of:

   a. names and addresses of the inhabitants of the town _____

   b. furniture in, for example, a house that is to be furnished _____

   c. goods for sale through the post _____

2. Choose the noun that means:

   a. a person who carts goods by road _____

   b. an express messenger _____

3. Choose the noun meaning an investigation:

   a. by a scientist to discover new truth _____

   b. by a mechanic of a car to see if everything is roadworthy _____

   c. by law officers to ascertain facts, especially in a case of death by suspected violence _____

4. Choose a noun that means a container for:

   a. a sword _____

   b. a small quantity of liquid medicine _____

   c. an archer's arrows _____

5. Choose a noun that means an introduction to:

   a. a stage play _____

   b. a book stating its scope and purpose _____

   c. a speech or legal document _____

© Valerie Marett
Coroneos Publications

Australian Homeschooling #562
Successful English 8A

Review Sentences

There are 4 main types of sentences: statements, questions, commands and exclamations. In addition there are greetings and responses.

Statements

- May communicate an observation, e.g., There are a lot of clouds today.
- They may communicate an inference, i.e. something found out by reasoning, e.g., It will probably rain presently.
- They may communicate judgement, e.g., Apollo Bay is the most restful place I know.

Questions

- They may seek to elicit a direct answer, e.g., Did you take a holiday last year?
- They may express doubt, e.g., Do you think I should go?
- They may seek to gain unreasoning acceptance of a judgement. these are called rhetorical questions and require no answer, e.g., Is there anyone so blind that they can not see what our next step must be?

Exclamations

These are used to express strong feelings in the most direct way, e.g., What a disaster!

Greetings

Greetings are an additional type of sentence needed to cover any conversational greeting not in the normal form of a statement or question, e.g., Hello! All the best! Good morning.

Responses

Responses are an additional type of sentence needed to cover any sentence that comes in response to what has been said. A response is completely dependent on what has been said, takes its whole shape from it and is often meaningless except in relation to it.

- They may indicate the listener is paying attention, e.g., Yes I see. Really.
- They may indicate whether the listener agrees or disagrees e.g., That's right. I don't think so.
- They may express any other response or answer not in the form of a normal statement or exclamation e.g., I hope so. Certainly.
- They make the response to conventional greetings, e.g., Quite well thanks. Good morning.

Identify each type of sentence. Make sure your answer is complete.

1. (Mary:) Congratulations, Barbara!

_____

2. (Barbara): Thank you, Mary.

_____

3. What is the capital of Peru?

_____

4. Rubbish!

_____

5. Peter has dirty marks all over his face.

_____

6. Let me know within the next few days.

_____

7. Don't forget to drop in next time you are passing this way.

_____

8. He's a passenger and should not be counted in the team.

_____

9. Dare I ask him?

_____

10. Just a minute, please

_____

11. Be quiet!

_____

12. Well I never!

_____

13. Need I tell you what a fine job he has done?

_____

14. She must be blushing at all the flattering remarks I made.

_____

15. Good!

_____

Review Conjunctions

A conjunction joins two single words, two phrases or two clauses. Sometimes a conjunction comprises a small phrase that acts as if it were a single word, e.g., so that, in order to, as if, even though.

A. Rewrite each sentence using the conjunction in the box to complete the sentences below. You may use each conjunction only once.

since	while	until	if	because

1. Andrew was unsuccessful. He wasted so much time.

   _____

2. They arrived. I was still eating breakfast.

   _____

3. I can not buy a bicycle. I have saved more money.

   _____

4. Nearly a month has passed. I received your letter.

   _____

5. John will play. You will play too.

   _____

B. Complete each sentence with a suitable conjunction:

1. I have not seen him _____ the end of term.

2. _____ it rained we did not get wet.

3. Mr Bruce will take a rest _____ his match.

C. Underline the conjunction in each sentence below.

1. Across the beach and into the sea ran the children.

2. He jumped out of the frying pan but into the fire.

3. Return the book when you have finished it.

4. In order to pass the course you must hand in all of your assignments and have references that indicate you have completed the necessary hours in a crèche.

Choosing the Right Word

A word is missing from each of the following sentences. In each case choose the correct word from the word in the brackets.

1. It was an act of _____ bravery. (incredulous, incredible)

2. In spite of their defeat the _____ of the team remained high. (morale, moral)

3. The crocodile had a _____ appetite. (veracious, voracious)

4. To save his son, the man had to _____ with his life. (gamble, gambol)

5. The ranger condemned the _____ capture of protected fauna. (illicit, elicit)

6. We did not _____ the speed limit. (exceed, accede)

7. Michael remained optimistic in the face of _____. (adversary, adversity)

8. The girl was the _____ swimmer in the lake. (soul, sole)

9. The alligator heading towards the dog was a horrible _____. (sight, site)

10. The witness gave a _____account of the incident. (veracious, voracious)

11. A business should choose a solution to a problem that is both _____ and correct for the business. (morale, moral)

12. The lookout on the Titanic was at first _____ when he sighted the large iceberg. (incredulous, incredible)

13. The giant was a terrifying _____. (adversary, adversity)

14. We could not _____ to your request to have the footpath the other side of the road. (exceed, accede)

15. The _____ for the new factory has been approved. (site, sight)

16. On reaching the beach we found there wasn't another _____ in sight. (soul, sole)

17. The woman was on _____ at the time. (vocation, vacation)

© Valerie Marett
Coroneos Publications

Australian Homeschooling #562
Successful English 8A

Development of Medieval Towns

The earliest centres of commerce were in the areas where agricultural production lagged behind the increase of population. Venice led the southern revival of trade and was closely followed by other Italian and southern French seaports, which could not feed themselves. Their survival depended on trade because these cities were not agriculturally self-sufficient. Further north in Flanders, the Rhineland, Northern France and the British Isles commercial revival also began in areas that were not self-sufficient.

The luxury trade played only a small part in the north compared with the Mediterranean commerce, but contact with the East was maintained through the hazardous route through the Gulf of Finland down through the River Dneiper to the Black or Caspian Seas. Overland trade was both dangerous and costly. Apart from the actual cost of transportation there was the expense of satisfying the feudal lords along the way who claimed the right to charge tolls to merchants passing through their lands and who would not hesitate to seize the merchant's goods if they were in urgent need of money.

The revival of commerce was the direct cause of the revival of towns. No important trade route could exist without towns and every great town arose on a trade route. The early merchants were the first settlers in what came to be urban communities in the Middle Ages. Although the merchants never constituted the majority of the population of any town their settlement drew to the town the small shopkeepers, drivers, carters, artisans and labourers whose livelihood depended upon the existence of large-scale trade.

Merchants needed three conditions for success. They needed a base of operation strategically located along trade routes, near local markets that were favourably situated for warehousing, transporting or transhipping goods. They required security in the form of protection by a strong, local power against the dangers of war or violent seizure of property by lawless elements in the feudal world. Finally they required freedom of movement and freedom from restrictions of the manorial peasantry.

Some of the important new towns that had been cities under the Roman Empire, like London, Paris and Cologne, were now revived after centuries of decline. Others towns grew up where a ruler or great feudal lord had built a castle or fortified strong point such as King Alfred of England who built "burhs" or those of a tenth century king in Germany called "burgen." Almost without exception the former Roman cities and tenth century military towns favourably located grew into towns whose inhabitants lived by trade and industry rather than by husbandry and bearing arms.

The earliest mercantile towns grew up outside the fortified areas as there was no room within. During the 11th and 12th century the growing towns built new walls to surround these enlarged areas. The same pattern appeared with those towns that grew up outside great monasteries or a royal manor. The protection provided by the king, abbot or lord provided the incentive for settlement and as the new town grew it eventually enveloped the monastery or manorial centre.

Answer these questions:

1. Where did the earliest centres of trade begin?

   _____

   _____

2. Think! Why would luxury trade have played a greater part in the Mediterranean than in the north?

   _____

   _____

   _____

   _____

3. What was it that led to the revival of towns? Why?

   _____

   _____

   _____

   _____

4. List the three conditions merchants needed for success.

   _____

   _____

   _____

   _____

   _____

   _____

   _____

5. Complete: The earliest mercantile towns grew up _____ areas. During the 11th and 12th century the growing towns built _____ these enlarged are as. Eventually the settlement _____ the monastery or manorial settlement.

6. Think! The town wall provided protection but it had another function. What would that have been?

   _____

English Poetry Through the Ages: Victorian Poetry

The Victorian era was a great period of great political, social and economic change. The Empire, recovering from the loss of the American colonies, entered a period of rapid expansion. This was combined with increasing industrialisation and mechanisation and led to a prolonged period of economic growth.

The major Victorian poets were Alfred, Lord Tennyson; Robert Browning; Elizabeth Barrett Browning, Matthew Arnold and Gerald Manley Hopkins.

The following poem, "The Charge of the Light Brigade," by Alfred, Lord Tennyson records a disastrous military engagement during the initial phase of the Crimean War fought between Turkey and Russia between 1854-56. Under the command of Lord Raglan the British forces entered the war in September 1854 to prevent Russia from obtaining control of the important sea routes through the Dardanelles. From the beginning the war was plagued with a series of misunderstandings and technical blunders, one of which is described in this poem.

Lord Raglan issued orders to the Light Brigade to prevent the Russians seizing guns from the British. Lord Raglan had intended to send the Light Brigade to pursue and harry a retreating Russian artillery brigade near the front line. Instead the Light Brigade was sent to make a frontal assault against a different artillery battery that was well prepared and with excellent defensive fire. The brigade over-ran its objective and was forced to retreat.

The poem, "The Charge of the Light Brigade" published six weeks after the event emphasizes the valour of the cavalry in bravely carrying out their orders.

The Charge of the Light Brigade

Half a league, half a league,
Half a league onward,
All in the valley of Death
Rode the six hundred.
'Forward, the Light Brigade!
Charge for the guns!' he said:
Into the valley of Death
Rode the six hundred.

'Forward, the Light Brigade!'
Was there a man dismay'd?
Not tho' the soldier knew
Someone had blunder'd:
Their's not to make reply,
Their's not to reason why,
Their's but to do and die:
Into the valley of Death

Cannon to right of them,
Cannon to left of them,
Cannon in front of them
Volley'd and thunder'd;
Storm'd at with shot and shell,
Boldly they rode and well,
Into the jaws of Death,
Into the mouth of Hell
Rode the six hundred.

Flash'd all their sabres bare,
Flash'd as they turn'd in air
Sabring the gunners there,
Charging an army, while
All the world wonder'd:
Plunged in the battery-smoke
Right thro' the line they broke;
Cossack and Russian
Reel'd from the sabre-stroke
Shatter'd and sunder'd.
Then they rode back, but not
Not the six hundred.

Cannon to right of them,
Cannon to left of them,
Cannon behind them
Volley'd and thunder'd;
Storm'd at with shot and shell,
While horse and hero fell,
They that had fought so well
Came thro' the jaws of Death,
Back from the mouth of Hell,
All that was left of them,
Left of six hundred.

When can their glory fade ?
O the wild charge they made!
All the world wonder'd.
Honour the charge they made!
Honour the Light Brigade,
Noble six hundred!

Each line in this poem is in dimeter. This means it has two stressed syllables which are followed by two unstressed syllables making the rhythm. Read the poem aloud so you can hear it.

Answer these questions:

1. How many lines in each verse?

   _____

2. Notice how the same rhyme, and occasionally the same word, is used for several consecutive lines. Give an example. Explain how this adds to the poem.

   _____

   _____

   _____

3. Give at least one reason
   Why you think Alfred, Lord Tennyson wrote this poem?

   _____

   _____

The following poem by Robert Browning has no historical basis. The action is supposed to have taken place in the early seventeenth century when some of the Dutch states banded together against the tyrannical power of Phillip II of Spain. Three men hasten to bring good tidings to Aix but only one gets there and we are not told what the news is—perhaps that the besieged town of Aix has been saved.

Note the breathless rhythm—the hurry of headlong lines, the steady beat of hoofs, the forward beat of the horses—which makes it obvious this ride is a matter of life and death.

How They Brought the Good News from Ghent to Aix

I sprang to the stirrup, and Joris, and he;
I galloped, Dirck galloped, we galloped all three;
'Good speed!' cried the watch, as the gate-bolts undrew;
'Speed!' echoed the wall to us galloping through;
Behind shut the postern, the lights sank to rest,
And into the midnight we galloped abreast.

Not a word to each other; we kept the great pace
Neck by neck, stride by stride, never changing our place;
I turned in my saddle and made its girths tight,
Then shortened each stirrup, and set the pique right,
Rebuckled the cheek-strap, chained slacker the bit,
Nor galloped less steadily Roland a whit.

'Twas moonset at starting; but while we drew near
Lokeren, the cocks crew and twilight dawned clear;
At Boom, a great yellow star came out to see;
At Düffeld, 'twas morning as plain as could be;

At Boom, a great yellow star came out to see;
At Düffeld, 'twas morning as plain as could be;
And from Mecheln church-steeple we heard the half-chime,
So Joris broke silence with 'Yet there is time!'

At Aerschot, up leaped of a sudden the sun,
And against him the cattle stood black every one,
To stare through the mist at us galloping past,
And I saw my stout galloper Roland at last,
With resolute shoulders, each butting away
The haze, as some bluff river headland its spray.

And his low head and crest, just one sharp ear bent back
For my voice, and the other pricked out on his track;
And one eye's black intelligence,—ever that glance
O'er its white edge at me, his own master, askance!
And the thick heavy spume-flakes which aye and anon
His fierce lips shook upwards in galloping on.

By Hasselt, Dirck groaned; and cried Joris, 'Stay spur!
Your Roos galloped bravely, the fault's not in her,
We'll remember at Aix'—for one heard the quick wheeze
Of her chest, saw the stretched neck and staggering knees,
And sunk tail, and horrible heave of the flank,
As down on her haunches she shuddered and sank.

So we were left galloping, Joris and I,
Past Looz and past Tongres, no cloud in the sky;
The broad sun above laughed a pitiless laugh,
'Neath our feet broke the brittle bright stubble like chaff;
Till over by Dalhem a dome-spire sprang white,
And 'Gallop,' gasped Joris, 'for Aix is in sight!'

'How they'll greet us!'—and all in a moment his roan
Rolled neck and croup over, lay dead as a stone;
And there was my Roland to bear the whole weight
Of the news which alone could save Aix from her fate,
With his nostrils like pits full of blood to the brim,
And with circles of red for his eye-sockets' rim.

Then I cast loose my buffcoat, each holster let fall,
Shook off both my jack-boots, let go belt and all,
Stood up in the stirrup, leaned, patted his ear,
Called my Roland his pet-name, my horse without peer;
Clapped my hands, laughed and sang, any noise, bad or good,
Till at length into Aix Roland galloped and stood.

And all I remember is, friends flocking round
As I sat with his head 'twixt my knees on the ground;
And no voice but was praising this Roland of mine,
As I poured down his throat our last measure of wine,
Which (the burgesses voted by common consent)
Was no more than his due who brought good news from Ghent.

© Valerie Marett
Coroneos Publications

Australian Homeschooling #562
Successful English 8A

Answer these questions:

1. Explain the meaning of the following in relation to the poem:

   a. postern: _____

   b. girth: _____

   c. spume-flakes:_____

   d. neck and croup over: _____

   e. buffcoat: _____

2. Explain how Browning has given us the feeling that a lot of time is passing.

   _____

   _____

   _____

3. What were the other two riders names? What happened to them?

   _____

   _____

4. What was the name of the storyteller's horse?

   _____

5. Think! Why did the story teller, towards the end of the poem throw away his coat and as much else as he could?

   _____

   _____

Further Work:

Another poem by Robert Browning is "The Pied Piper of Hamlyn." This poem is a fable that ends with a moral about what can happen if a person does not keep their promises.

1. Find and read the poem.

2. Look up the meaning of any words or expressions you do not understand.

3. Summarise the story contained in the poem.

4. State briefly any theories as to what actual event this poem was written about.

The Correct Word in the Correct Place

Use the words in the box at the top to complete each sentence. Use a dictionary if you are not sure of the exact meaning of the words. It will help if you first group together the words in the box with similar meaning on a piece of paper.

> adapt, implicit, beneficial, ostensible, tantamount, extricate, punctilious, continuously, negligent, deprecated, beneficent, ostentatious, paramount, depreciated, intricate, adopt, punctual, negligible, explicit, continually

1. He admitted that his driving had been _____, but claimed that the damage that had resulted had been _____.

2. The matter was so _____ that he found it hard to _____ himself.

3. Though a despot he was a _____ one, and made many laws that were _____ to his people.

4. His arrival was _____ and he carried out his duties with _____ regard to detail.

5. It rained _____ last week, one storm lasting _____ for as long as four hours.

6. He emphasised that it was of _____ importance to recognise if we consulted the university professor, it was be _____ to recognising him as the leading authority on obscure dialects.

7. He _____ the proposal that the Australian dollar should be deliberately _____, since his income would then be worth less.

8. Though he did not state this as an _____ fact, I think we can assume that it was _____ in what he said.

9. The _____ reason for giving the party was to welcome the visitors from abroad, but the real reason was to allow him to make an _____ display of his wealth.

10. You will be able to _____ yourself to any situation if you _____ measures appropriate to the situation.

Important Definitions

Read the following definitions carefully:

Alliteration: the systematic repetition of the same sound in a piece of writing to produce a certain effect, sometimes humorous.,
For example, Larry's lizard likes leaping leopards.

Anti-climax: this happens when the build up to a climax is spoilt or made to look ridiculous by a sudden descent to something quite trifling,
For example, In the sudden assault on the city he lost his brother, father, both his legs and his purse.

Antithesis: any arrangement of words to emphasize the meaning by contrast. In the following example the man's inner worry is emphasized by contrasting it with his outward calm.
'He wandered along with an indifferent look on his face but with a heart eaten away by care.'

Cliché: any stale or overworked expression is called a cliché.
For example, it is important to engage your audience.

Couplet: any two lines of rhyming verse, especially when of equal length.
For example, I am the dog world's best detective,
　　　　　My sleuthing nose is so effective.

Epigram: any piece of wisdom concisely or wittily expressed. A proverb is an epigram that has been taken up by the common people and has endured a long time.
For example, a stitch in time saves nine.

Epitaph: an inscription on a tombstone,
For example. Here lies my wife: here let her lie!
　　　　　Now let her rest, and so am I.　　(John Dryden)

Fable: if a short story is merely a cover for teaching a moral it is called a fable. The fable of the tortoise and the hare is not really about animals but about the moral that slow but steady wins the race.

Irony: this is any gentle form of sarcasm in which the opposite of what is said is really meant.
For example, the procrastinator's meeting has been postponed.

Spoonerism: We are said to commit a spoonerism when we accidentally change the position of letters in words so that what is meant to be serious sound ridiculous.
For example, for smooth riding give me a well-boiled icicle. (well-oiled bicycle)

Look at each example below. Decide which definition best fits and write it in the space provided.

1. Deciding to travel, he left his family, his house and his tortoise.

   _____

2. Sometimes I'm tired of all these rooms
   Kept very clean with mops and brooms.

   _____

3. Round the rugged rock the ragged rascal ran.

   _____

4. A little learning is a dangerous thing.

   _____

5. The boy said he thought the poem was written by either Sheats or Kelly.

   _____

6. He's a wonderful batsman; he misses everything.

   _____

7. This be the verse you grave for me:
   Here he lies where he longed to be;
   Home is the sailor, home from the sea,
   And the hunter home from the hill.

   _____

8. We must learn to live together as brothers or perish as fools.

   _____

9. It's as good as gold.

   _____

10. The ant worked all summer long gathering food. The grasshopper lazed and danced thinking he must start to work tomorrow. When winter came the ant was snug in his home with plenty of food. The grasshopper came begging at the door. The ant told him to laze and dance all winter too.

   _____

11. Here lies John Dentist, filling his last cavity.

   _____

Review of Subject & Predicate

The subject of the sentence is who or what the thing is about.
The predicate is the part of the sentence that makes a statement about the subject and contains the verb.
For example, The man from Adelaide met us on the way home.
>   Subject: The man from Adelaide   Predicate: met us on the way home.

Look at each sentence. Decide which is the subject and predicate. Write it in the box provided lower down the page.

1. How do they make pottery?

2. John threw the ball over my head.

3. Round the corner galloped a runaway pony.

4. Come quickly!

5. The man came to our rescue when we called for help.

6. What an extraordinary athlete Dawn Fraser was.

7. My brother shaves when he gets up in the morning.

8. Someone has purposely removed it.

9. I will go providing it is fine.

Subject	Predicate

Review of the Objective Case

The objective case is the form of the noun or pronoun used in the predicate. To find the noun in the objective case ask "who" or "what" after the verb. It is the object in the sentence.

For example: Frank is a happy little boy.

subject—Frank   verb—**is**

is who or what— a happy little boy

Look at each sentence. Decide which is the subject, predicate and object. Write them in the box provided lower down the page. Underline the verb. Be careful! Find the simple sentence first.

1. That boy likes brown sugar.

2. He who pays the piper calls the tune.

3. Men with beards have many female admirers.

4. The girl who lives there won a university scholarship.

5. They disguised themselves so that they should not be recognised.

6. His sister mended his trousers with great skill.

7. Roger finished the homework set by his teacher.

8. Did anyone see anything?

Subject	Predicate	Object

© Valerie Marett
Coroneos Publications

Australian Homeschooling #562
Successful English 8A

The Revolt of the Towns

The towns, through their manufacture and trade, were the wealthiest members of the feudal system, so the lords looked to them for money when they were in need. These demands eventually became unendurable and a long struggle arose between the lords and the townsfolk, which resulted in the enfranchisement of the towns.

By the eleventh century the townsfolk had strengthened their walls, learnt to fight and had become bold enough to defy their lords and shut their gates in the face of tax collectors and even in the face of the lord or king himself. This contest lasted for two centuries or more. The merchants banded together and were collectively able to resist the exactions and control the movement and sale of goods. This meant that uncooperative lords lost the profits of tolls and customs. The lords were forced to extend liberties and franchises for the first time to the non-noble population of Europe as a result of the economic pressure which merchants, associated together in guilds could bring to bear on them.

The liberties obtained by the merchants consisted of specific and particular privileges and exemptions rather than general freedoms. Merchants, like the peasants, never became social or legal equals of the nobility, whose freedom was qualified only by the restrictions or obligations specified by feudal custom.

The earliest bourgeois liberties were almost entirely economic and social rather than political. Self-government of towns outside Italy was generally a development that came after the twelfth century. However, gradually, the greater number of towns of Western Europe either bought with money, or wrested by force of arms, charters from the lords. These charters varied, but they all incorporated certain basic liberties. Foremost among these was the free status of the inhabitants of the town, a condition guaranteed by the legal provision that any inhabitants who could prove residence for a year and a day within the town was accepted as a free person. It also granted the right to buy, sell or lease land within the town; exemption from labour services owed by the peasants; the substitution of fixed money rents due to the lord of the town, and the right to sue and be sued only in urban court—a court which adjudicated according to the customs of the town.

Lords who granted these liberties found the rights given by charter were more than made than paid for by the profits. Merchants paid heavily for the charters; tolls and customs collected by the lords grew as a result of increased trade; the profits of the lord's neighbouring manors increased because of the growing markets for agricultural products created by growing towns.

As the cities, under the protection of their charters, grew in wealth and population many of them became strong enough at last to cast off actual dependence on the lord or king and became, in effect, independent states. This was especially true in the case of the Italian cities and, in a less marked degree, some of the German towns.

A. Answer these questions:

1. How were towns viewed by lords originally, as their wealth increased?

   _____

2. What caused changes in the lords attitude?

   _____

   _____

   _____

   _____

3. What were the earliest liberties obtained by the towns under charters?

   _____

   _____

   _____

   _____

   _____

   _____

4. How did lords who granted these charters benefit?

   _____

   _____

5. What happened eventually as the towns grew in strength?

   _____

   _____

B. Word Knowledge: choose the correct word from the text to fit the meaning below.

1. belonging to or characteristic of the middle class   _____

2. to endow with the right of citizenship   _____

3. the authority extended to an individual or group
   to carry out specific commercial activities   _____

C. Grammar: find the subject, predicate and object in the sentence below.

The towns were the wealthiest members of the feudal system.

_____

English Poetry Through the Ages: Twentieth Century Poets

William Butler Yates and Thomas Hardy were poets who bridged the Victorian era and the twentieth century. As poetry changed to modernist they adapted.

Some poets of the twentieth century still continued to use traditional structures and forms, whiles other rejected it completely. Poems became shorter, more precise and a less ornate style was preferred. After 1945 the postmodern movement brought more abstract and experimental styles of poetry.

Some of the main poets of this era include Walter de la Mare, Robert Frost, T.S. Elliot, Robert Graves, D.H. Lawrence, Stephen Spender, Cecil Day-Lewis and Dylan Thomas.

The following poem by Walter de la Mare, "Silver," is probably the best poem ever written on the effects of moonlight on countryside.

Read the poem carefully then answer the questions.

Silver

Slowly, silently, now the moon
Walks the night in her silver shoon;
This way, and that, she peers, and sees
Silver fruit upon silver trees;
One by one the casements catch
Her beams beneath the silvery thatch;
Couched in his kennel, like a log,
With paws of silver sleeps the dog;
From their shadowy cote the white breasts peep
Of doves in silver feathered sleep
A harvest mouse goes scampering by,
With silver claws, and silver eye;
And moveless fish in the water gleam,
By silver reeds in a silver stream.

1. The poem rhymes in _____.

2. In the poem the moon is _____.

3. What are the only things moving in the poem? How does this add to the effect?

_____

_____

The next poem is by William Butler Yeats. On an autumn day he walks down a woodland park to a lake where the same swans he has watched for nineteen years are swimming. In this poem he depicts the natural world as being pristine and ever-beautiful, especially as viewed in contrast with human nature.

The Wild Swans at Coole

The trees are in their autumn beauty,
The woodland paths are dry,
Under the October twilight the water
Mirrors a still sky;
Upon the brimming water among the stones
Are nine-and-fifty swans.

The nineteenth autumn has come upon me
Since I first made my count;
I saw, before I had well finished,
All suddenly mount
And scatter wheeling in great broken rings
Upon their clamorous wings.

I have looked upon those brilliant creatures,
And now my heart is sore.
All's changed since I, hearing at twilight,
The first time on this shore,
The bell-beat of their wings above my head,
Trod with a lighter tread.

Unwearied still, lover by lover,
They paddle in the cold
Companionable streams or climb the air;
Their hearts have not grown old;
Passion or conquest, wander where they will,
Attend upon them still.

But now they drift on the still water,
Mysterious, beautiful;
Among what rushes will they build,
By what lake's edge or pool
Delight men's eyes when I awake some day
To find they have flown away?

1. What do you learn from the poem about the swans?

_____

_____

_____

_____

2. There are three themes in this poem. Name and explain them.

_____

_____

_____

Modernist poetry is hard to understand so only one example will be shown below. The poem is by Ezra Pound, who is considered to be the greatest of the modernists. He believed in: a direct treatment of a thing, whether subjective or objective and avoiding vague generalities; the use of no words that did not contribute to the presentation; he rejected conventional metrical form in favour of individualised cadence.

A Song Of The Degrees

I
Rest me with Chinese colours,
For I think the glass is evil.

II
The wind moves above the wheat-
With a silver crashing,
A thin war of metal.

I have known the golden disc,
I have seen it melting above me.
I have known the stone-bright place,
The hall of clear colours.

III
O glass subtly evil, O confusion of colours !
O light bound and bent in, soul of the captive,
Why am I warned? Why am I sent away?
Why is your glitter full of curious mistrust?
O glass subtle and cunning, O powdery gold!
O filaments of amber, two-faced iridescence!

Malapropism

A malapropism is a ridiculous misuse of a word, especially in mistake for one resembling it.

Each of the sentences below contains a malapropism, which is shown in bold. Replace it with the correct word from the box.

> credible, emphatic, exhort, masticate, prodigy,
> bannister, debut, sportsmanship, pinnacle, optimist,
> sonatas, invention, vacated, forceps

1. The actor's **debacle** _____ at the age of seventeen was acclaimed by critics and public alike.

2. Seats on the District Council had to be **vaccinated** _____ every three years.

3. Beethoven was an infant **progeny** _____; he composed three **tomatoes** _____ before he was four years old.

4. My fiancé is at the very **pineapple** _____ of her career.

5. Mr Micawber, a Dickens character, was a born **octopus** _____ always expecting something to turn up.

6. His denial of the charges was so **erratic** _____ that everyone believed him.

7. Necessity is the mother of **intervention** _____.

8. The speaker told the pupils that he could not too strongly **exhaust** _____ them to play fairly in the true spirit of **sportiveness** _____.

9. The doctor was so hard up he had to pawn his **biceps** _____.

10. Some of the adventures he claimed to have had were so strange they were hardly **creditable** _____.

11. You will have indigestion if you do not **emasculate** _____ your food properly.

12. The boy speedily reached the bottom of the stairs by sliding down the **barristers** _____.

Main and Subordinate Clauses

A main clause is a sentence that contains at least a subject and a predicate and can stand alone as a complete sentence. For example, She ate the cakes.

Subordinate clauses can not stand alone. It will begin with a subordinate conjunction or relative pronoun and will contain both subject and verb. It can describe nouns and pronouns; describe verbs, adverbs and adjectives; or act as the subject or object of another clause.

For example: Even though the day was warm and sunny, the man refused to get up.

Main clause: the man refused to get up

Subordinate clause: even though the day was warm

Subordinate conjunctions: after, although, as, because, before, even if, even though, if, in order that, once, provided that, rather than, since, so that, than, that, though, unless, until, when, whenever, where, whereas, wherever, whether, while, why.

Relative conjunctions: that, which, whichever, who, whoever, whom, whose, whosoever, whomever.

A. Look at each sentence below. Identify the main clause and subordinate clause and write them in the appropriate place.

1. The car, that broke down on the freeway, was fifteen years old.

   Main clause: _____

   Subordinate clause: _____

2. Since he was so late he missed the opening speech.

   Main clause: _____

   Subordinate clause: _____

3. My sister and I were at Grandma's house when my mother rang me to come and collect her.

   Main clause: _____

   Subordinate clause: _____

4. I like to eat lunch outside when the sun is shining.

   Main clause: _____

   Subordinate clause: _____

© Valerie Marett
Coroneos Publications

Australian Homeschooling #562
Successful English 8A

5. Since his car broke down Mr Johnson rides the bus to work.

    Main clause: _____

    Subordinate clause: _____

6. The mouse ran through the kitchen and ate the bread while the family slept.

    Main clause:(2) _____

    _____

    Subordinate clause: _____

7. Unless you have another idea, we will play Monopoly this afternoon.

    Main clause: _____

    Subordinate clause: _____

8. Magicians often perform tricks which appear impossible.

    Main clause: _____

    Subordinate clause: _____

9. Pets, who are properly trained, act obediently.

    Main clause: _____

    Subordinate clause: _____

10. Mandy cooked a casserole which was declicious.

    Main clause: _____

    Subordinate clause: _____

11. After eating his meal, David paid the bill.

    Main clause: _____

    Subordinate clause: _____

12. After John caught the fish, Kelly caught one also.

    Main clause: _____

    Subordinate clause: _____

© Valerie Marett
Coroneos Publications

Australian Homeschooling #562
Successful English 8A

The Industrial Life of the Towns

The towns were the workshops of the late Middle Ages. The most important characteristics of these towns were the guilds. Almost as soon as the towns organised themselves, the great merchants came together and formed guilds.

Their main aim was to preserve a monopoly of all trades for themselves. The monopoly was strengthened with the rise of larger business transactions after the eleventh century and it usually followed that town councillors and the major magistrates were members of the merchant guilds or their nominees. These guilds soon became strong enough to bargain with Kings, especially when they were asked to lend money to the Crown.

The merchant guilds had an unchecked monopoly of trade within their respective towns and supervised all crafts. They punished bad workers or those using inferior material; they prevented price cutting and made fixed arrangements for the prices of raw material and finished products. The guilds also controlled the fairs and markets and dictated the terms on which an outsider could trade with their towns. They had some judicial powers in settling trade disputes and often used these powers to strengthen their monopoly. In effect they closed their towns to all those not under their control.

Every man traded as a member of a Guild and these guilds effectively controlled the towns. When the control of the merchant guilds became too exacting the discontented workers in each craft tended to meet secretly and discuss their wrongs. The end result of this was the creation of separate workers guilds or craft guilds such as those of the goldsmiths, bakers, fishmongers, weavers etc. Sometimes there were as many as fifty of these associations while large cities like London and Paris had more than one hundred craft guilds.

The craft guilds soon found that union gave them strength and their meetings of apprentices, journeymen and masters discussed every question concerning their own craft, and, later the life of the town. As they grew the craft guilds became increasingly jealous of their reputations. By the fourteenth century they were ousting the merchant guilds from their privileged positions.

Within the guilds were a small number of masters who were owners of their homes and sold the goods there. The master had a certain number of apprentices whose usual term for apprenticeship was seven years. The master also employed a certain number of journeymen, or men paid by the day. These journeymen were independent while the apprentices had to stay with the master and be lodged, fed and clothed by him. After his apprenticeship a man could hire himself out as a journeyman but he could not become a master until he had submitted to the guild inspectors a piece known as a "master-piece."

Craft guilds covered relief work among the members of their dependents in times of illness or death. They held frequent social gatherings and supervised the morals and conduct of their members.

© Valerie Marett
Coroneos Publications

Australian Homeschooling #562
Successful English 8A

Craft guilds objected to the political monopoly maintained by the merchants and demanded a share in government. Sometimes this was arranged peacefully and sometimes after a revolt but gradually they won a place beside the merchants in governing the town.

A. Think carefully then answer these questions fully:

1. What was the purpose of the merchant guilds?

_____

_____

_____

_____

2. What was the purpose of craft guilds?

_____

_____

_____

3. Explain in your own words the differences between masters, apprentices and journeymen?

_____

_____

_____

_____

4. What had to happen before a journeyman could become a master?

_____

_____

_____

B. Word Knowledge: find a word from the text that fits the following definition

1. the total ownership or control of something _____

2. to push out from their position _____

C. Identify the main and subordinate clause in the sentence below.

Masters owned homes and sold goods there.

_____

English Poetry Through the Ages: World War 1 Poets

During both World Wars poets emerged from among those fighting and so much of the poetry is about the patriotism they felt and the circumstances they found themselves in. During World War 1 the most famous poets were Rupert Brooke and Owen Seaman.

The poem below is written by Rupert Brooke and is an extremely famous poem written in 1914. British soldiers were often buried in French national cemeteries and there is a huge field full of white crosses dedicated to soldiers whose names were unknown.

The Soldier

If I should die, think only this of me:
That there's some corner of a foreign field
That is for ever England. There shall be
In that rich earth a richer dust concealed;
A dust whom England bore, shaped, made aware,
Gave, once, her flowers to love, her ways to roam,
A body of England's, breathing English air,
Washed by the rivers, blest by suns of home.
And think, this heart, all evil shed away,
A pulse in the eternal mind, no less
Gives somewhere back the thoughts by England given;
Her sights and sounds; dreams happy as her day;
And laughter, learnt of friends; and gentleness,
In hearts at peace, under an English heaven.

Think, then answer the questions:

1. What is the poem saying?

_____

_____

_____

_____

2. What is this type of short poem called?

_____

This poem "Pro Patria" by Owen Seaman shows much about the nationalist fervour of those who went to fight and those left at home and the sacrifices they were called to make.

England, in this great fight to which you go
Because, where Honour calls you, go you must,
Be glad, whatever comes, at least to know
You have your quarrel just.

Peace was your care; before the nations' bar
Her cause you pleaded and her ends you sought;
But not for her sake, being what you are,
Could you be bribed and bought.

Others may spurn the pledge of land to land,
May with the brute sword stain a gallant past;
But by the seal to which you set your hand,
Thank God, you still stand fast!

Forth, then, to front that peril of the deep
With smiling lips and in your eyes the light,
Steadfast and confident, of those who keep
Their storied scutcheon bright.

And we, whose burden is to watch and wait--
High-hearted ever, strong in faith and prayer,
We ask what offering we may consecrate,
What humble service share.

To steel our souls against the lust of ease;
To find our welfare in the common good;
To hold together, merging all degrees
In one wide brotherhood;--

To teach that he who saves himself is lost;
To bear in silence though our hearts may bleed;
To spend ourselves, and never count the cost,
For others' greater need;--

To go our quiet ways, subdued and sane;
To hush all vulgar clamour of the street;
With level calm to face alike the strain
Of triumph or defeat;--

This be our part, for so we serve you best,
So best confirm their prowess and their pride,
Your warrior sons, to whom in this high test
Our fortunes we confide.

Answer these questions:

1. Does the poem on the previous page show the contrast with the desire for peace and the patriotism that drove men to fight when they believed the cause was just? Explain and give examples.

_____

_____

_____

_____

2. What do you think "to bear in silence though our hearts may bleed" refers to?

_____

_____

Further Work:

Write a Persuasive Essay discussing the following: The Anzac Legend: What is it? How was it created? Why is it important we remember it?

Follow all the rules of writing. Attach your essay below.

© Valerie Marett
Coroneos Publications

Australian Homeschooling #562
Successful English 8A

Words Using Latin Prefixes

Often one word can effectively replace several. Choose a word containing a Latin prefix from the box to fit each meaning. Use your dictionary if you are not sure of the meaning of the words.

recondite, disseminate, exculpate, erudite, omnivorous, circumlocution, omnipotent, preamble, disingenuous, excoriate, antediluvian, intransigent, discursive, decrepit, permeate, avert, expulsion, incursion

1. before the flood; very ancient   _____

2. to turn away; prevent

   _____

3. very learned

   _____

4. worn out through old age   _____

5. saying in many words what might be said in a few   _____

6. going from one point to another without very much planning   _____

7. to scatter or spread about   _____

8. not sincere or frank   _____

9. to take the skin off, especially of human beings

   _____

10. not allowing the entrance of   _____

11. refusing to compromise   _____

12. to free from all blame   _____

13. hidden or hard to understand   _____

14. eating all kinds of food   _____

15. a sudden invasion or attack, with no intention of staying any time   _____

16. all knowing   _____

17. to filter or drain slowly through   _____

18. an introduction, especially to a legal document   _____

© Valerie Marett
Coroneos Publications

Australian Homeschooling #562
Successful English 8A

Using a Single Word Instead of Many

Rewrite the sentences below, substituting a single word for the words that are underlined. Choose from the words in the box. Use a dictionary if you are not sure.

> exhumed, convalescent, silhouette, amphibious, substantiate, intestate, sinecure, insolvent, irrelevant, biennially, octogenarian

1. My uncle is a <u>man who has lived eighty years.</u>

   _____

2. Frogs are <u>able to live on land as well as water.</u>

   _____

3. He holds a <u>position in which he is well paid for doing practically nothing.</u>

   _____

4. After pneumonia he is now <u>gradually recovering his health.</u>

   _____

5. This event occurs <u>once every two years.</u>

   _____

6. This artist is expert at making <u>blocked outlines of faces as seen from the side.</u>

   _____

7. Mr Jones died <u>without having made a will.</u>

   _____

8. Can you <u>give a good reason to prove</u> your claim?

   _____

9. In this prosperous country, there are not many tradesmen <u>who are unable to pay their debts.</u>

   _____

10. The body was <u>removed from the grave for examination.</u>

    _____

11. The chairman ruled that the point raised was <u>without bearing on the matter under discussion.</u>

    _____

Condensed Sentences

We can often make one word do instead of several if we know :

- **the correct technical term,** e.g., Hamlet often speaks aloud his thoughts when no-one is present **or** Hamlet often soliloquizes

- **if the item is a list belonging to one class of things,** e.g., Mum put sheets, pillow-cases, tablecloths and serviettes to soak **or** Mum put the linen to soak.

- **we omit a word that repeats another,** e.g., One of the two halves was put away in a box **or** one half was put in a box.

- **a single word can often be found to express the full meaning of a phrase or clause,** e.g., After an interval of several minutes he returned (phrase) **or** presently he returned. Our visitor, who is a native of Britain, is going to speak to us (clause) **or** our British visitor is going to talk to us.

- **if a single word can not be found to replace a clause a short phrase sometimes can,** e.g., He rarely drives when he has to use his headlights **or** he rarely drives after dark.

- **Occasionally we can save words by finding an entirely different way of expressing things,** I had already emailed a reply when your email arrived **or** our emails crossed.

- **Many verbose Latinisms can be shortened by using shorter Anglo Saxon ones,** e.g., in the vicinity **or** nearby; surface abrasion **or** graze; the financially underprivileged or the poor.

Condense the following:

1. Help me put away the cups, saucers, plates and bowls.

2. The weather is unexpected considering the season.

3. When the cold weather returns, deciduous trees lose their leaves.

4. He spoke with mild anger.

5. The ball landed on the smooth stretch of turf between the tee and putting green.

6. Always answer emails by the end of the day.

7. The old man looked as happy as a schoolboy in a well stocked pantry.

Figures of Speech and Poetic Devices

Do you remember these terms on page 34 and 78?

A Simile: in a simile we compare one thing with a generally unlike thing in order to emphasise the quality which it has in common with other things.

A Metaphor: a metaphor makes a comparison between two unlike things. It states that a thing **is** something other than what it is.

Hyperbole: a hyperbole is an exaggeration aimed at making one's words more effective. The words are not meant to be taken literally: they are figurative.

A pun: a pun is a play on words, that is, a statement that is made surprising and amusing by using a word that can have two meanings.

Onomatopoeia: this is the name given to language when the words attempt to help the meaning through the sound.

Personification: this takes place whenever some object or abstract idea is spoken of as if it was a person. We are apt to personify a ship by referring to it as "she."

Alliteration: the systematic repetition of the same sound in a piece of writing to produce a certain effect, sometimes humerous.

Epigram: any piece of wisdom concisely or wittily expressed. A proverb is an epigram that has been taken up by the common people and has endured a long time.

The following statements are expressed in the form of similes. They could be more forceful if they were compressed into metaphors shortening the number of words used.

For example: We shall find ourselves in difficulties like a non-swimmer in deep water.
We shall find ourselves in deep water.

Rewrite each sentence changing the similes into metaphors.

1. We are both sharing the same risk, like two men in the same boat.

   _____

2. He is a wicked man, and is like an apple that is rotten to the core.

   _____

3. It makes me feel as though my flesh is creeping.

   _____

A. Which sentence contains a metaphor? Underline the metaphor.

1. The disappointment broke her heart.
   The sudden jolt broke his arm.

2. The mother watches the young bird as it flies from its nest.
   At the slightest difficulty Janet flies to her mother.

3. The minutes crept slowly by.
   The cat crept stealthily towards the mouse.

B. Change the similes contained in these sentences to metaphors.

1. I was so startled I felt like my heart was in my mouth.

   _____

2. You have things the wrong way round, just as though you were putting the cart before the horse.

   _____

3. We are wasting time like a man flogging a dead horse.

   _____

C. State whether each sentence contains personification, hyperbole, pun, epigram, onomatopoeia, alliteration, metaphor or simile.

1. Duty is what one expects from others. _____

2. Beyond the last lone lamp I passed. _____

3. And all I ask is a tall ship and a star to steer her by. _____

4. The robbers rained blows upon him. _____

5. The doctor asked the priest if he thought life was
   worth living. The vicar replied that it depended
   on the liver. _____

6. I heard the ripples washing in the reeds
   And the wild water lapping on the crag. _____

7. It rained cats and dogs all day. _____

8. It makes me feel as though my flesh is creeping. _____

9. My heart was in my mouth. _____

Adjectival Clauses

Adjectival clauses do the work of adjectives. They add meaning to nouns. Adjectival clauses begin with relative pronouns. The relative pronouns are <u>who, whose, whom, which, what</u> and <u>that</u>. <u>When</u> may also introduce an adjectival clause when it stands instead of "during which" or "on which." Occasionally the relative pronoun is understood or implied.

For example: This is the brown horse <u>that won last year's Derby</u>.
Adjectival clause

Here's the coffee flavour <u>I like</u>. (that is implied)
Adjectival clause

Read the sentence. Write the adjectival clause in the space provided. Circle the noun it modifies.

1. A theatre is a place where plays are performed.
   _____

2. Do you remember the year when Alice was married?
   _____

3. The moment that he entered was marked by a sudden hush.
   _____

4. The boy, whose cat you found, is very grateful.
   _____

5. Is that the dress that you bought?
   _____

6. Where is the girl who was standing beside you?
   _____

7. Jack and Johnathon attend the class which meets on Thursday.
   _____

8. The rose is the flower which was selected.
   _____

9. Billy is the friend whom you helped.
   _____

A. Combine the pair of sentences by changing the underlined sentence to an adjectival clause.

1. A wren was trying to build a nest. <u>It had been injured.</u>

   _____

2. This is the building. <u>I go to school.</u>

   _____

3. Aunt Pauline is my mother's sister. <u>She will visit us in June.</u>

   _____

4. Do you remember the name of the man? <u>The man you met</u>.

   _____

5. She is the one. <u>She thought of the idea.</u>

   _____

B. Underline the adjectival clause. Write the main clause on the line provided.

1. Tammy likes the same books that you like.

   _____

2. Anyone who wishes to leave early may do so.

   _____

3. The man, whose wife teaches English, is a tennis professional.

   _____

4. He is not the sort of person to whom I would entrust a secret.

   _____

5. This is the book I was telling you about.

   _____

C. Make a complex sentence by supplying the main clause for each adjectival clause below.

1. who called a few minutes ago

   _____

2. when the result is announced

   _____

© Valerie Marett
Coroneos Publications

The Lombard League

Economic revival stimulated the growth of trade and ultimately the development of towns. These towns were largely economic and social organisations and most did not achieve political authority. Where they did gain political power it was mostly by force, which was commonly exercised by a sworn alliance of townsmen or a "commune." These first appeared in Italy where the united guilds formed the Lombard League that forced Frederick Barbarossa, the holy Roman Emperor, to yield them independence in 1183.

In Italy the medieval towns acquired their greatest power becoming prosperous through trade with the East and from the enormous impetus given to their power by the Crusades. With wealth came power and all the chief Italian cities became distinct self-governing states with just a nominal dependence on the Pope or Emperor. The main towns in the Lombard League were Milan, which was situated where the Alpine trade converged; the manufacturing city of Florence, which was famous for its cloths, brocades, metal beating and jewellery—a city of art and banking, a stronghold of guild; the port of Genoa which had an unrivalled position for trading with the Black Sea and the Orient; Pisa, the rival of Florence in banking and trade; and Venice, which the Crusades had made the greatest trading post of the Mediterranean and the most cosmopolitan medieval town.

The city states of Italy were constantly at war with one another. By the end of the thirteenth century many of the town's democratic institutions were overthrown and had fallen into the hands of domestic tyrants, e.g., Florence fell into the hands of the Medici. Some of these despots rendered themselves odious by their crimes but many, who were rich and powerful through trading enterprises, were enlightened rulers and extended patronage to artists and scholars, liberally prosecuted public works and added glory to their particular city by the splendour of their courts.

The system of banking developed by these towns added another important contribution to the world. In the Middle Ages, the Church forbad usury, or the lending of money at interest, so the business of money lending fell into the hands of the Jews. The Jews became the leading capitalists of the time and paid various kings to protect them. They were hated everywhere and expelled from certain countries, so, as the northern Italian towns had become the financial centres of the world those Jews living there became the bankers of the world and gradually extended their influence over all Europe. They were referred to as "Lombards" and bargained with wasteful kings to secure privileges.

The Lombards established themselves in all countries and both politically and economically extended their operations to become a regular international system. They accepted deposits, arranged for these to be transferred from one account to another in payment of commercial debts and even allowed customers to overdraw their accounts. Gradually they arranged for "bills of exchange" to take place without the dangerous transport of gold. So an international system of credit and exchange was built up and this made further expansion of trade possible. The Lombards gave the world its international economic system. This system of trade has changed little and still goes on.

Australian Homeschooling #562
Successful English 8A

A. Word Knowledge: find a word from the text that fits the following definition.

1. impulse, stimulus _____

2. the lending of money at interest _____

3. an economic system in which all major
   decisions as to the production and
   distribution of goods and services are made
   by private individuals and business
   firms with a minimum of government intervention _____

4. belonging to all parts of the world; free from local
   ideas of national ideas of loyalties _____

B. Think, then answer these questions.

1. How did a few of the towns manage to gain political power?

   _____

   _____

2. In what country were the towns with the greatest political power and
   therefore independence found?

   _____

3. What advantage did the towns in that country have over some of the other
   European towns?

   _____

   _____

4. List the main towns in the Lombard League.

   _____

5. What had happened to the government of many of the towns by the
   thirteenth century?

   _____

   _____

6. Why were the Jews left to run the banking system?

   _____

   _____

7. What functions did these banking institutions undertake?

   _____

English Poetry Through the Ages: World War 2 Poets

War is not pretty and causes a huge loss of life. You will see this reflected in the poems below. The first poem, written by Laurence Binyon, describes how the country was affected by the loss.

For the Fallen

With proud thanksgiving, a mother for her children,
England mourns for her dead across the sea.
Flesh of her flesh they were, spirit of her spirit,
Fallen in the cause of the free.
Solemn the drums thrill; Death august and royal
Sings sorrow up into immortal spheres,
There is music in the midst of desolation
And a glory that shines upon our tears.

They went with songs to the battle, they were young,
Straight of limb, true of eye, steady and aglow.
They were staunch to the end against odds uncounted;
They fell with their faces to the foe.

They shall grow not old, as we that are left grow old:
Age shall not weary them, nor the years condemn.
At the going down of the sun and in the morning
We will remember them.

They mingle not with their laughing comrades again;
They sit no more at familiar tables of home;
They have no lot in our labor of the day-time;
They sleep beyond England's foam.

But where our desires are and our hopes profound,
Felt as a well-spring that is hidden from sight,
To the innermost heart of their own land they are known
As the stars are known to the Night;
As the stars that shall be bright when we are dust,
Moving in marches upon the heavenly plain;
As the stars that are starry in the time of our darkness,
To the end, to the end, they remain.

Answer these questions:

1. What three things have been personified?

_____

2. Describe how each of these three things have been personified.

_____

_____

3. Explain the imagery that has been used in verse two and the words used to convey this.

_____

_____

4. Read verse 3 carefully. These four lines are regularly used by R.S.L. Clubs and on Anzac Day to commemorate the fallen.

The first poem "For the Fallen" is much quieter in mood than the next poem by Gunner W. S. T. Stacey that reflects the noise of battle, especially of the large guns firing. The "sight and bubble run" describes an inbuilt spirit level in the gun.

The Thunder of the Guns

Like the storm that's in the making
When the rumbling thunder runs
And the hills and valleys tremble:
That's THE THUNDER OF THE GUNS.

When the aiming posts are planted
And the firing order comes,
Then the layers work their magic
With their sight and bubble runs.

Then the check is on the charges
And the range that's on the drum,
Then the muzzle flashes lightning:
That's THE THUNDER OF THE GUNS.

It's in the fury of the battle
When the understanding comes
That the gunner is forever,
A partner with the guns.

With the smoking breaches empty
And the dust and cordite gone,
There's a rumble in the distance:
That's THE THUNDER OF THE GUNS.

The Gods of War have finished
And the Sands of Time have run,
But always there's the memory of
THE THUNDER OF THE GUNS.

And as today becomes the future
Our sons will tell their sons,
That the men whose blood they carry:
Knew THE THUNDER OF THE GUNS.

In the valley of the shadows
When his comrades are as one,
Their hearts will surely gladden
For they're the only ones
That understand the music:
In THE THUNDER OF THE GUNS.

Answer these questions:

1. To what does the poet liken the sound of guns? What figure of speech is used?

   _____

   _____

2. Why do you think the gunner is described as being a "partner with his guns"?

   _____

   _____

3. Later in the poem two quite vivid metaphors are used. Identify them and write them below.

   _____

   _____

4. When were guns likely have been "music" to people?

   _____

   _____

5. Why do you think "the thunder of the Guns" is written in capitals and repeated at the end of many verses?

   _____

   _____

The Holocaust was the mass murder of six million Jews under Hitler along with many other peoples, e.g., the gypsies, who were considered "subhuman. Not surprisingly some war poems were written about this.

The following is a famous poem written by Martin Niemoller, a Protestant Pastor. Read it carefully as it is still relevant today.

In Germany they first came for the Communists,
and I didn't speak up because I wasn't a Communist.
Then they came for the Jews,
and I didn't speak up because I wasn't a Jew.
Then they came for the trade unionists,
and I didn't speak up because I wasn't a trade unionist.
Then they came for the Catholics,
and I didn't speak up because I was a Protestant.
Then they came for me—
and by that time no one was left to speak up.

Answer the question:

What is the theme of this poem?

_____

_____

Holocaust

We played, we laughed
we were loved.
We were ripped from the arms of our
parents and thrown into the fire.
We were nothing more than children.
We had a future.
We were going to be doctors, lawyers,
rabbis, wives, teachers, mothers.
We had dreams, then we had no hope.
We were taken away in the dead of night
like cattle in cars, no air to breathe smothering,
crying, starving, dying.
Separated from the world to be no more.
From the ashes, hear our plea.
This atrocity to mankind can not happen again.
Remember us, for we were the children
whose dreams and lives were stolen away.

- Barbara Sonek

Answer this question:

The previous poem, "Holocaust," is a stark reminder of the reality of the Holocaust. Think about what the poem is really saying and write your thoughts below.

_____

_____

_____

_____

Review the various ages of English poetry you have visited while working through this book. Decide which of these ages you enjoyed the most or which of the poets you enjoyed most. Summarise your reasons and write them below including names of poems, quotes from them and poet's names, if applicable.

_____

_____

_____

_____

_____

_____

_____

_____

_____

_____

_____

_____

_____

_____

_____

_____

_____

_____

_____

_____

_____

Revision—Nouns

A. Use a collective noun to complete each phrase below.

1. a _____ of books

2. a _____ of flowers

3. a _____ of cars

4. a _____ of wolves

5. a _____ of tools

6. a _____ of steps

7. a _____ of bees

8. a _____ of thieves

B. Write a noun listing a small quantity of something, e.g., a splinter of wood.

1. an _____ of energy

2. a _____ of grass

3. a _____ of glass

4. a _____ of rain

C. Add –sion, —ance, —cy, —tion or —ness to make an abstract noun.

1. decide _____

2. surly _____

3. isolate _____

4. repentant _____

5. explode _____

6. erupt _____

D. Write the correct abstract noun to fit each definition below.

1. the state of being able to meet difficult situations without fear _____

2. the state of being thankful _____

3. the quality of companionship and sharing unity of interest _____

4. the act of urging someone by advice or reason to do something _____

E. List four examples of nouns that are neuter gender.

1. _____   2. _____   3. _____   4. _____

F. Name the nouns and pronouns that are common gender.

_____

_____

© Valerie Marett
Coroneos Publications

Australian Homeschooling #562
Successful English 8A

Revision—Correct Word, Correct Ending

A. Choose the correct word in brackets that means the same as the word or words in the first column.

1. reference   (allusion, illusion)   _____

2. to influence   (effect, affect)   _____

3. bearing or appearance   (mean, mien)   _____

4. standing still   (stationery, stationary)   _____

5. despicable   (contemptuous, contemptible) _____

B. Name the person below who.....

1. builds with stone   _____

2. climbs tall buildings to make repairs etc.   _____

3. drives a motor car for a living   _____

4. sets glass in window frames   _____

5. engages in the business of selling lollies or chocolates   _____

C. Complete each entence below by adding "—ary, —ery, —ceed,—cede, —sede ,—cy, —sy, —efy" or "—ify."

1. The South wished to se_____ from the Union.

2. The artill_____ group received a medal.

3. The witness will now be called to test____.

4. There was no vacan_____ at the inn the night Jesus was born.

5. Can a democra_____ have too much bureaucra____?

6. Maybe Mum will inter_____ for us when Dad sees the broken window.

7. If reasoning does not suc_____ with the children I may need to resort to brib____.

8. For me, the taste of chocolate is sheer ecsta_____.

Revision: Verbs

A. Write the verb and say if it is transitive or intransitive.

1. The children sang many songs.

   _____

2. They were home before they were expected.

   _____

3. The boy laughed very loudly.

   _____

B. identify the verb in each sentence below and state its tense.

1. I noticed the weather was growing worse.

   _____

2. The girl says she prefers a young horse.

   _____

3. The streets will be deserted by the time we pass through them.

   _____

C. Identify the noun or nouns and verb or verbs in each sentence. Write them on the line provided. (You may include pronouns.)

1. The explorers reached a deserted cabin that was badly in need of repair.

   _____

2. I can not trust you as I trusted John.

   _____

3. Aunt Debbie know a cosy restaurant where excellent meals are served.

   _____

4. She ran so quickly that she soon overtook the others.

   _____

5. Although it is raining heavily I must catch the train.

Revision: French Words and Phrases

English contains many words of French origin that have become Anglicised over the years, e.g., machine, force, police, routine.

Match the definition to the correct word or phrase in the box. Learn what you do not know.

> resume; tete-a-tete; applique; nom de plume; boutique;
> a la carte; fait accompli; repertoire; au fait; debut; vinaigrette;
> façade; a la mode; sabotage; premiere; bon appetit

1. subversive destruction _____

2 first public performance of an entertainment
   group or personality _____

3. a fake persona _____

4. first public performance of play or film _____

5. author's pseudonym _____

6. an intimate get together or private conversation
   between two people _____

7. salad dressing of oil or vinegar _____

8. being conversant in or with, or instructed with _____

9. a document listing ones qualifications for a job _____

10. individual dishes ordered rather than a fixed price meal_____

11. an inlaid or decorative feature _____

12. an accomplished fact; something that has already
    happened and is unlikely to be repeated _____

13. a clothing store, usually selling designer clothes rather
    than mass produced clothes _____

14. good appetite; enjoy your meal _____

15. a body of items regularly performed _____

16. fashionable _____

© Valerie Marett
Coroneos Publications

Australian Homeschooling #562
Successful English 8A

Revision: Adjectives

A. Adjectives may be divided into six main classes. Look at each sentence below. Say which class each of the underlined adjectives belongs. State the noun it qualifies.

1. I should like **this cream** cake please.

   _____

2. **Neither** girl knew **which** way to go to reach the station.

   _____

3. The **hardest** day of the race will be the **sixth** and **last** day.

   _____

4. **My** cat was chased down the street by **that** dog.

   _____

B. Rewrite the sentences below, substituting a single adjective from the box for each underlined phrase. Be careful, you may need to rearrange the sentence.
For example, We noticed several houses **in which nobody lives.**
We noticed several uninhabited houses.

squalid, impenetrable, lowering, vigilant, unceremonious, spruce

1. The morning sky was **overcast and threatening.**

   _____

2. Businessmen usually look **neat in dress and appearance.**

   _____

3. A good guard has to be **constantly on watch.**

   _____

4. The explorer came to a mountain **that could not be crossed.**

   _____

5. The visitor behaved in a manner **that was informal and rather abrupt, even a little discourteous.**

   _____

6. The room looked **dirty, mean and poor.**

   _____

Revision: Figures of Speech

Say if the following are example of a simile, metaphor, hyperbole, pun, onomatopoeia, alliteration, or personification.

1. He was as old as the hills. _____

2. Santa's helpers are subordinate Clauses. _____

3. Chug, chug, chug the train puffed up the hill. _____

4. I slept like a log last night. _____

5. She did not realise that opportunity was knocking at her door. _____

6. I'm getting married in the morning
   Ding dong the bells are going to chime. _____

7. The wheels of justice turn slowly. _____

8. Nature reserves are an eagle opportunity employer. _____

9. Time creeps up on you. _____

10. The lesson was taking forever. _____

11. Her hope was a fragile seed. _____

12. Sara's seven sisters slept soundly in the sand. _____

13. He smoked like a chimney. _____

14. Pop, pop, fizz, fizz,
    Oh what a relief it is!   (Alka Seltza slogan) _____

15. Time flew, so before we knew it, it was time to return home. _____

16. My teeth were chattering as I waited in the cold for the bus to arrive. _____

17. Laura's lizard likes leaping leopards. _____

18. I will die if he asks me to dance. _____

19. The wheels of justice turn slowly but they grind exceedingly small. _____

Revision: Adverbs

A. Look at each sentence. State whether the adverb in bold in each sentence modifies a verb, an adjective or an adverb.

1. This house is **quite** large. _____

2. You are **quite** right about that car. _____

3. She spoke **extremely** loudly. _____

4. Mary sings **beautifully**. _____

5. David is **extremely** smart. _____

6. This car goes **incredibly** fast. _____

B. Underline the adverb and state whether it is an adverb of manner, time or place.

1. He spoke quietly to the agitated horse. _____

2. We leave tomorrow on our trip to Thailand. _____

3. I live here. David lives in the next street. _____

4. Peter is standing near your nephew. _____

5. The plumber solved the problem of the leaking tap easily. _____

6. My guest, Olivia, arrived yesterday. She was early. _____

7. Janette is still waiting for her brother to come out of the shop. _____

8. Joel stayed behind to help clean the hall after the party. _____

9. He drove the car carefully out of the garage. _____

10. I will read the rest of the story to you later. _____

11. Marcus rarely rings anymore. He emails instead. _____

12. She sang loudly in the shower. _____

© Valerie Marett
Coroneos Publications

Australian Homeschooling #562
Successful English 8A

More French Words and Phrases Used in English

Match the definition to the correct word or phrase in the box. Learn what you do not know.

> café au lait, maître d', faux pas, protégé, par excellence, attache haute coutre, piece de resistance, en route, cordon bleu, au fait en suite, hors d'oeuvre, potpourri, petit four, matinee, déjà vu,

1. high class, expensive clothing style _____

2. master of the dining room _____

3. an outstanding accomplishment or the final part of something _____

4. a feeling you have that you have already seen or done something when you haven't _____

5. a foolish mistake, something that shouldn't be done _____

6. on the way _____

7. coffee with milk _____

8. a scented mixture of dried flowers and spices; a miscellaneous group or collection _____

9. an appetiser before the main meal _____

10. a small desert, particularly a cake _____

11. someone whose training is sponsored by an influential person _____

12. person assigned to a diplomatic post _____

13. "blue ribbon" in cookery, Master Chef _____

14. preeminent, the best _____

15. the day's first showing of a play _____

16. part of a set, together, often used to refer to a small bathroom joined to a bedroom _____

17. conversant with, informed _____

Revision: Common Figurative Expressions

Choose a figurative expression from the box at the bottom to fit each meaning. Write it on the line.

1. a reserve method of action in case the first fails _____

2. not to seek revenge for an injury _____

3. to extract and make use of another's ideas _____

4. a subject that leads to bitter arguments _____

5. a subject that causes keen and general discussion _____

6. to avoid being friendly with someone _____

7. an unwanted person causing trouble in the group _____

8. to call attention to one's own good qualities _____

9. to like being seen, heard and noticed by the public _____

10. to give someone information necessary to understand what is happening _____

11. to waste time adding to something of which there is already ample _____

12. that reminds me of something I have heard before _____

13. close together, side by side _____

14. to cause people to quarrel _____

to carry coal to Newcastle	to put someone in the picture
a burning question	to set people by the ears
to keep someone at arm's length	that rings a bell
to blow one's own trumpet	cheek by jowl
a bone of contention	a second string to one's bow
to be fond of the limelight	to pick someone's brain
to turn the other cheek	a cuckoo in the nest

© Valerie Marett
Coroneos Publications

Australian Homeschooling #562
Successful English 8A

Revision: Pronouns

There are nine main classes of pronouns: personal, impersonal, relative, interrogative, reflexive, possessive, distributive, demonstrative, and indefinite. For each sentence, on the space provided write the pronoun and say what class it is.

1. Neither accusation is true. _____

2. It is so cold it is snowing in the mountains. _____

3. I like curling up in front of a fire on a cold day. _____

4. None of these old clothes are worth keeping. _____

5. Joel is going to the shops to buy himself a bottle of soft drink. _____

6. The tree had lost all of its leaves by winter. _____

7. She wanted that much soil for the garden. _____

8. Several of us have suggested cancelling the meeting today. _____

9. The person who gains the highest score will win the scholarship. _____

10. What is that on your blouse? _____

11. The car, which hit mine, was very old. _____

12. This is heavier than that. _____

13. I saw myself reflected in the mirror above the fireplace. _____

14. Someone has stolen the leg of lamb. _____

15. John can run very fast but he does not swim. _____

16. It is dangerous to play with fire. _____

17. Everything he touches seems to turn to gold. _____

18. Whose pen is this? _____

© Valerie Marett
Coroneos Publications

Australian Homeschooling #562
Successful English 8A

Revision: Prepositions

A. Look at each sentence below. Study each underlined preposition. State:

- **what noun or noun equivalent it governs**
- **what phrase it introduces**
- **between what two words it shows the relationship.**

1. My grandfather did not approve of girls with short hair.

   _____

2. This parcel looks quite different from the last one.

   _____

3. Television in colour is relatively new.

   _____

4. I believe he is in the next room.

   _____

B. Insert the correct preposition in the following sentences.

1. You will need to account _____ any money you spend _____ the treasurer.

2. Divide the cake _____ the adults and the lollies _____ the two children.

3. The number of items must correspond _____ the invoice.

4. Do not intrude _____ a matter that does not concern you.

5. I must part _____ some of the things I own as I am moving to a smaller house.

6. The Liberals argued _____ a national referendum to include Councils in the Constitution.

7. John has been entrusted _____ carrying the flag in the parade.

8. If the trousers are not the right size for Tom you can exchange them _____ a larger pair.

9. I wish to inquire _____ the progress of my printing.

10. Mum has agreed _____ tutor our next door neighbour's son.

Revision: Removing Ambiguity

It is important to write correctly so there is no ambiguity. Ambiguity is doubt or uncertainty regarding what the writer intended in either words, pictures or other media. Text speak is an excellent example of ambiguity.

Rewrite the following sentences so the meaning becomes clear.

1. The young child entered the room that just been painted in his best clothes.
   _____

2. Having fallen asleep, my friend said I began to talk in my dreams.
   _____

3. Professor Bright has been doing research on human behaviour in the University of Western Australia.
   _____
   _____

4. I remember, as a boy, buying a number of white mice which emptied my money-box.
   _____

5. Try our hot pies! You'll n ever get better.
   _____

6. He meant nothing less than to insult her.
   _____

7. The teacher told him to be quiet in a loud voice.
   _____

8. He was angry with his brothers for blaming his children, especially James.
   _____

9. Not long afterwards came the potato famine, and this of course was the Irishman's staple diet.
   _____
   _____

© Valerie Marett
Coroneos Publications

Australian Homeschooling #562
Successful English 8A

Revision: Identify Sentences

There are 4 main types of sentences: statements, questions, commands and exclamations. In addition there are greetings and responses. These can all be broken down into further groups.

Identify each type of sentence. Make sure your answer is complete, e.g., What is the capital of Peru? This a question seeking to elicit a direct answer. **There are fourteen groups. 11 are used below. Use each only once.**

1. Hello James. How are you today?

   _____

2. Quite well thanks and you?

   _____

3. It looks like we might get snow tonight.

   _____

4. Take your feet off that table.

   _____

5. Should I lose some weight?

   _____

6. You look so beautiful!

   _____

7. Exactly.

   _____

8. The new tax is no good for anyone.

   _____

9. Are you children all deaf?

   _____

10. Goodness, I hope so.

    _____

11. Please help with the canteen if you can.

    _____

Revision Subject, Predicate and Object

Look at each sentence. Decide which is the subject, predicate and object. Write them in the box provided lower down the page. Underline the verb. Be careful! Find the simple sentence first.

1. Mark and I played basketball.

2. Reading and learning can be fun activities.

3. Do you want to eat pasta or pizza?

4. I read a book and ate a box of chocolate.

5. John, Mark, Jacob and Luke ate waffles.

6. Frank ate waffles, bacon, toast and potatoes.

7. Doug and David washed and waxed the car.

8. My Mum told me, "Your sister is at the park."

9. I rode my bike while Jan ran down the street.

10. Tennis and football are both popular sports.

Subject	Predicate	Object

© Valerie Marett
Coroneos Publications

Australian Homeschooling #562
Successful English 8A

Important Definitions

Look at each example below. Decide which of the following terms best fits and write it in the space provided: alliteration, anticlimax, antithesis, cliché, couplet, epigram, epitaph, fable, irony, spoonerism.

1. His smile spoke friendliness; his secret thoughts were of undying hatred.

   _____

2. A certain man on entering his pew at church said, "I am occupewing my pie.

   _____

3. You're a fine friend. Why, you desert me at first sign of danger.

   _____

4. A perpetual holiday is a good definition of hell.

   _____

5. The bombs utterly destroyed the power station, the cathedral, the airport, the hospital and several dustbins.

   _____

6. To grass, or leaf, or fruit, or wall

   _____

7. Peter Piper picked a peck of pickled pepper.

   _____

8. Rover was a true friend: always loyal, ready to please and wagging his tail.

   _____

9. Look before you leap.

   _____

10. The hares were so persecuted by other animals that they ran away when anyone came. One day they saw a troop of wild horses and ran into the lake determined to drown themselves. But just as they got to the bank, a troop of frogs, frightened in their turn, jumped into the water. (There is always someone worse off than you.)

    _____

Main and Subordinate Clauses

A. **Look at each sentence below. Identify the main clause and subordinate clause and write them in the appropriate place.**

1. If Krystal goes to the shops she will be late for music practise.

   Main clause: _____

   Subordinate clause: _____

2. On his birthday Adam received a football which he traded for a cricket bat.

   Main clause: _____

   Subordinate clause: _____

3. We were watching TV on the couch and eating sandwiches.

   Main clause: _____

   Subordinate clause: _____

4. Kim likes listening to her iPod which is pink.

   Main clause: _____

   Subordinate clause: _____

5. The dog barked at the burglar who was stealing the computer.

   Main clause: _____

   Subordinate clause: _____

6. Since Suzanne likes to ride horses we have joined a pony club.

   Main clause: _____

   Subordinate clause: _____

7. Mother cooked a casserole which was delicious.

   Main clause: _____

   Subordinate clause: _____

Revision:Malapropisms

A malapropism is a ridiculous misuse of a word, especially in mistake for one resembling it.

Each of the sentences below contains a malapropism, which is shown in bold. Replace it with the correct word from the box.

circumnavigate, moss, prostrate, influence, bated, voracious, dissension, equilateral, punctual, evacuate, crustaceans, fait accompli, contradiction, proceed, photographic, stature

1. We will *precede* _____ now we have all arrived. You lead the way.

2. Being *punctuate* _____ means being on time.

3. The flood was so bad they had to *evaporate* _____ the city.

4. I find it easy to remember as I have a *photogenic* _____ memory.

5. Joseph said he could not eat crab or other *Asians* _____.

6. A rolling stone gathers no *moths* _____.

7. I can not help you as my *affluence* _____ over my niece is very small.

8. The teacher asked who was the first Englishman to *circumvent* _____ the globe.

9. I waited her arrival with *baited* _____ breath.

10. Politicians often try to create **dysentery** _____ among their opponents ranks.

11. He was a man of great *statue* _____.

12. I can assert the truth of it without fear of *contraception* _____.

13. She had a *veracious* _____ appetite.

14. I could not change his mind. It was *Fiat accompli* _____.

15. I was *prostate* _____ with grief.

16. A triangle whose sides are equal is called an *equatorial* _____ triangle.

Words Using Latin Prefixes

Often one word can effectively replace several. Choose a Latin prefix from the box to fit each meaning. Use your dictionary if you are not sure of the meaning of the words.

> recondite, disseminate, exculpate, erudite, omnivorous, circumlocution, omnipotent, preamble, disingenuous, excoriate, antediluvian, intransigent, discursive, decrepit, permeate, avert, expulsion, incursion

1. saying in many words what might be said in a few _____

2. not allowing the entrance of _____

3. all knowing _____

4. before the flood; very ancient _____

5. refusing to compromise _____

6. to turn away; avert; ward off _____

7. a sudden invasion or attack, with no intention of staying any length of time _____

8. hidden or mysterious _____

9. worn out through old age _____

10. scatter or spread about _____

11. going from one point or subject to another without very much planning _____

12. not sincere or frank _____

13. eating all kinds of food _____

14. to filter or drain slowly through _____

15. to take the skin off, particularly of human beings _____

16. to free from blame _____

17. an introduction, especially to a legal document _____

18. very learned _____

Revision: Using a Single Word Instead of Many

Rewrite the sentences below, substituting a single word for the words that are underlined. Choose from the words in the box. Use a dictionary if you are not sure.

innocuous, immaterial, ambiguous, infallibility, procrastination, hostage, impecunious, intestate, rhetoric, impermeable, maritime

1. It was odd for a lawyer to die <u>without making a will.</u>

_____

2. Australia lacks interests <u>appertaining to the sea.</u>

_____

3. One of our men was held by the enemy as a <u>pledge for the fulfilment of an agreement.</u>

_____

4. He said that to him it was <u>of no great importance</u> whether he stayed or went.

_____

5. My friend's remark was <u>capable of more than one interpretation.</u>

_____

6. <u>The art of speaking to persuade</u> is often used unscrupulously.

_____

7. <u>The putting off things until later</u> is the thief of time.

_____

8. The manager's belief in his own <u>inability to do anything wrong</u> was at the root of his unpopularity.

_____

9. He jokingly said his brother was always <u>without money.</u>

_____

10. The speaker argued that a small amount of whatever you enjoyed <u>was unlikely to harm anyone.</u>

_____

11. Raincoats should be made from material <u>that won't let water through.</u>

_____

Revision: Figures of Speech and Poetic Devices

A. Change the similes contained in these sentences to metaphors.

1. Whatever I say to him is forgotten instantly, as though it had gone in one ear and out another.

   _____

2. She is dependent on her mother as though she was tied to her apron strings.

   _____

3. She is of such a generous nature that one might almost imagine her heart to be made of gold.

   _____

B. State whether each sentence contains personification, hyperbole, pun, epigram, onomatopoeia, alliteration, euphemism, metaphor or simile.

1. He ran like lightning. _____

2. Love rules her kingdom without a sword. _____

3. This notice appeared on the window of a photography shop: our business is developing. _____

4. I know not where the white road runs. _____

5. The great aircraft rose bird-like into the sky. _____

6. He swallowed the bait. _____

7. Vulgarity is the conduct of those we do not like. _____

8. How they tinkle, tinkle, tinkle,
   In the icy air of night!
   Keeping time, time, time
   In a sort of runic rhyme. _____

9. His clothes have seen better days. _____

10. He ran me off my legs. _____

11. Wisdom crieth without; he uttereth his voice in the street _____

© Valerie Marett
Coroneos Publications

Australian Homeschooling #562
Successful English 8A

Revision: Adjectival Clauses

A. Read the sentence. Write the adjectival clause in the space provided. Circle the noun it modifies.

1. I do not know the city which Jane mentioned.

   _____

2. The man that I saw was sitting on a wooden bench.

   _____

3. The weather, that followed the thunderstorm, was cool.

   _____

4. The time period when acting auditions will be held is almost over.

   _____

B. Combine the pair of sentences by changing the underlined sentence to an adjectival clause.

1. The woman is a registered nurse. She lives next door.

   _____

2. Summer starts next week. It is my favourite season.

   _____

3. The dog belongs to the Smiths. You found the dog.

   _____

4. This is the building. I learn dancing.

   _____

C. Underline the adjectival clause. Write the main clause on the line provided.

1. How do you like the flavour I picked out for you?

   _____

2. Unlike the organ, which dates back to Roman times, the piano is fairly modern.

   _____

3. Mary, whom I have known for twenty years, is leaving the district.

   _____

Answers Successful English 8A

Page 5
Reviewing Plural Nouns
1. mosquitoes
2. flies
3. galleries
4. quizzes
5. fungi
6. atlases
7. storeys
8. benches
9. pliers (only plural)
10. vertices
11. indexes
12. symphonies
13. mice
14. volcanoes
15. legislation (doesn't change)
16. potatoes
17. knives
18. gulfs
19. larvae
20. synopses
21. dictionaries
22. lice
23. ova
24. taxes
25. roofs
26. cacti
27. daughters-in-law
28. churches
29. bacteria
30. zoos
31. tomatoes
32. cattle (only plural)

Page 6
Review of Nouns
A. Collective Nouns
1. board
2. litter
3. queue
4. gang
5. chorus
6. quartet
7. century

B. Abstract Nouns
1. consciousness
2. radiance
3. intrusion
4. distortion
5. accuracy
6. allusion

C. Correct Abstract Noun
1. vigilance
2. conclusion
3. navigation
4. intrusion
5. encouragement

Page 7
A. Noun Gender Changes
1. sow
2. spinster
3. doe
4. mare
5. heiress
6. waitress
7. ewe
8. duchess
9. goose
10. bride

B. Nouns of common gender
1. people
2. poultry
3. horses

C. Noun of Quantity
1. speck
2. strand
3. drop
4. pinch
5. slice
6. breath

D. Word for a phrase
1. intersection
2. speculation

Page 9
A. Definition
1. feudum or fief
2. vassi dominici
3. fidelity
4. benefices
5. anarchy
6. hierarchy
7. revocable
8. serf

B. Answer the questions
1. Charles Martel was the first person to enlist soldiers as vassi dominici. He needed good soldiers and the offer of land in return for services provided an incentive for soldiers.

© Valerie Marett
Coroneos Publications

Australian Homeschooling #562
Successful English 8A

Answers Successful English 8A

2. The kings after Charlemagne were weak and civil war erupted resulting in anarchy.

3. The Vikings came from the Scandinavian countries, mostly Norway, Sweden and Denmark; the Moslem raiders came across the Mediterranean from Africa and up through Spain; the Magyar came from Hungary.

4. A freeman could become a soldier or a serf.

5. The greatest change was that grants or benefices were no longer revocable but became hereditary.

Page 11
Complete
1. Answers may vary. Examples:
   tide & beside
   field & shield
   gay & away
   devise & wise

2. a. **tourney:** a tournament between knights

   b. **joust:** a Medieval tournament on horseback where two knights fought on horses using lances and trying to unseat each other.

   c. **comliest:** most handsome

   d. **glee:** laughter

3. It lasted fifteen days.

Page 12
Answer the questions
1. A pilgrimage was a trip to a church or shrine to pray to for forgiveness for a sin or healing from a sickness.

2. They usually travelled in a group for protection. A group was less likely to be robbed.

3. It was spring. We know because the narrator mentions March and April, which are spring in England. (You can also tell by the narrator's description of the weather and the countryside.)

Page 13
4. Answers will vary. Suggestions:
   March & parch
   power & flower

5. a. showers
   b. sweet
   c. drought
   d. root
   e. vein
   f. flower

Research and write
Parent to check.

Page 14
A. —ary or —ery
1. voluntary   artillery   honorary
2. vocabulary   stationary   dictionary   necessary
3. bribery   stationery
4. sedentary   salutary
5. flattery   secondary

B. Complete word with —ceed, —cede or —sede
1. secede
2. accede
3. exceed
4. recede
5. supersede
6. precede
7. proceed
8. concede
9. succeed

C. —cy or —sy
1. vacancy
2. bankruptcy
3. heresy
4. literacy
5. democracy   bureaucracy

D. —efy or —ify
1. ratify
2. testify
3. putrefies
4. liquified

Page 15
Occupations
1. mason
2. plumber
3. florist
4. glazier
5. athlete
6. confectioner
7. sculptor

© Valerie Marett
Coroneos Publications

Australian Homeschooling #562
Successful English 8A

8. chauffeur

9. steeplejack
10. solicitor

Correct Word
1. affect
2. momentous
3. ingenious
4. mien
5. proceed
6. allusion
7. contemptible
8. legible

Page 16
A. Verb and Type
1. was broken (infinitive, past tense)

2. can cause (infinitive, present tense)
   dropping (present participle)

3. ran (finite)

B.
1. boiled   (intransitive)

2. write   (transitive) (subject is
   you, presumed)

3. sang (transitive) knew (non-finite)

Page 17
Nouns and verbs
1. gold Kalgoorlie (n) was discovered (v)

2. cars hill crest (n) came (v)

3. wreath flowers memorial (n) school's
   and war are used as adjectives
   was placed (v)

4. you he I friends (n) are (v)

5. spectator (n) screamed (v)

6. mother I my way (n)
   kissed hurried (v)

7. postman gate (n) opened (v)

8. it you school (n) is raining   go (v)

9. Mt Kosciusko tourists skiers scenery (n)
   is visited   like (v)

10. Krystal map she Australia (n)
    said had to draw (v)

11. Our teacher person (n) is(v)

12. creatures scrub (n) were darting (v)

13. I tea summer (n)   to drink (v)

Page 19
A. Answer the questions:
1. king, Tennants-in-Chief, vassals, serfs

2. The Tennants-in Chief had to appear,
   when called on with a fully armed army
   ready to fight. They were to attend the
   king's or Tennant-in-Chief's Court when
   summoned to give advice or help
   dispense justice. They had to pay money
   to the lord when they succeeded to the
   fief (death duties) and give extra money
   if their lord wanted to build a castle, go
   on a Crusade, be ransomed, at the
   knighting of the eldest son and the
   marriage of a daughter.

3. It was their responsibility to protect the
   kingdom or fiefdom, to give justice in
   vassals court and to respect the personal
   and family interests of the vassal.

4. A serf had to cultivate the fields for the
   lord and produce food, build bridges,
   mend roads and guard the overlords
   cattle. In return they were given a
   cottage and small strips of land to grow
   their own food on. They had the right to
   be protected by the lord and to take
   refuge in the castle keep in times of
   trouble.

5. Yes, when everyone carried out their
   responsibilities, but when vassals
   revolted, their overlords were helpless.

B. Word Knowledge
1. relief
2. apex
3. domain
4. retinue

C. Research
This is the code.
- To fear God and maintain His Church
- To serve the liege lord in valour and faith
- To protect the weak and defenceless
- To give succour to widows and orphans
- To refrain from the wanton giving of
  offence
- To live by honour and for glory
- To despise pecuniary reward
- To fight for the welfare of all
- To obey those placed in authority
- To guard the honour of fellow knights
- To eschew unfairness, meanness and
  deceit
- To keep faith

Answers Successful English 8A

- At all times to speak the truth
- To persevere to the end in any enterprise begun
- To respect the honour of women
- Never to refuse a challenge from an equal
- Never to turn the back upon a foe

Page 20
Answer these questions:

1. Answers will vary. Suggestions:
   peace   war;   burn   freeze;
   live   die;   perish   health;
   love   hate

Page 21

2. a. nothing
   b. escape
   c. in any way
   d. by own hand
   e. the cause
   f. problem

3. Answers may vary slightly. Suggestion. The poet has fallen in love and he describes the roller coaster of emotions he feels when the object of his love appears to notice him or ignores him.

Page 22
Answer the questions:

1. It is winter and bitterly cold. Icicles are hanging from the wall outside where water has dripped down and frozen. The milk has frozen in the milkmaids pail. The wind is blowing hard and there is a great deal of coughing in church.

2. Answers may vary slightly: The poet is saying that despite warm clothing people outside feel extremely cold and the roads are difficult to walk on, probably covered with snow that has either frozen and become slippery or is slushy.

3. a. stirs the pot
   b. the priests sermon
   c. birds have fluffed up their feathers against the wind

4. Answers will vary. Examples
   wall   hall   nail   pail

Page 23

5. It is either very late autumn or early. spring We know this because the poet speaks of "the darling buds of May",

that is the buds on the trees, being shaken by rough winds. May is late spring in Britain and June starts summer. It is probably the start of summer as he starts the poem by saying "shall I compare thee to a summers day."

6. quatrains

7. It could mean that the person will live on as long as the poem is read in the world, or if it was written about Elizabeth 1 it could mean her glory would never fade.

8. a. a lease is for a set period. It suggests that summer has a set period of 3 months.

   b. even tempered

   c. the sun

9. the sun   death

10. The theme is the stability of love and its power to immortalise the poetry and its subject.

Research
   Parent to check

Page 24
French Words and Phrases

1. a la carte
2. façade
3. nom de plume
4. repertoire
5. sabotage
6. fait accompli
7. tete-a-tete
8. vinaigrette
9. applique
10. a la mode
11. boutique
12. debut
13. premiere
14. resume
15. au fait
16. bon appetite

Page 25
A. Suffixes—Adjectives

1. dilatory   —ory
2. transitory   —ory
3. vindictive   —ive
4. skittish   —ish
5. derogatory   —ory
6. negligible   —ible
7. prostrate   —ate
8. insular   —ar

Answers Successful English 8A

B. Suffixes—Nouns
1. predecessor   —or
2. egotist   —ist
3. successor   —or
4. philatelist   —ist
5. slovenliness   —ness
6. vacancy   —cy
7. emulation   —tion
8. appropriateness   —ness
9. atheist   —ist

Page 26
Class of Adjective, Noun Qualified
1. fifth: numerical   candidate (n)
   my: possessive   cousin (n)
2. neither: distributive   boy (n)
   what: interrogative   homework (n)
3. these: demonstrative   loaves (n)
   fresh: descriptive
   loaves (n) (understood)
4. this: demonstrative   page (n)
   two: numerical   errors (n)
   serious: descriptive   errors (n)
   next: descriptivepublication (n)
5. which: interrogative   month (n)
   finest: descriptive   weather (n)
6. last: descriptive   question (n)
   sixth: numerical
   question (n) (understood)

Page 27
Change to an adjective
1. He was shipwrecked on an uninhabited island.
2. It was an unprecedented event.
3. She made an impromptu speech.
4. Being improvident, he did not provide for the future.
5. His appetite was gargantuan.
6. He was an unassuming child.
7. There was only a glimmering light.
8. The work of Shakespeare is likely to be immortal.
9. Old people sometimes become garrulous.
10. I took a blank piece of paper.
11. Wooden warships are obsolete.

Page 29
A. Word Knowledge
1. arable

2. rotation
3. latifundium
4. agrarian
5. economic unit

B. Answer the questions:
1. Most of the population was made up of peasants.
2. Medieval villages were loosely based on the great landed estates of the Romans.
3. The Roman landed estates grew more crops than they needed themselves and sold it for profit to the towns. By Medieval times towns had declined and so medieval villages grew only enough for their own population and became largely self-sufficient.
4. A typical village was made up of a few huts in which the peasants lived surrounded by land. The land was divided into two fields that were not fenced off.
5. No-one in the village was wealthy enough to be able to own oxen and plough therefore it was necessary for the village to combine their resources and their labour. This meant individual plots were inefficient.
6. There were two fields so the crops could be rotated, leaving one field fallow each year.
7. One of the reasons the yield was small was that the seeds were scattered by hand allowing the birds to eat much of the seed.

Page 30
Answer these questions
1. Death is personified in this poem. This means that Death has been treated like he was a real person.

Page 31
2. Answers will vary. Suggestion: Words like rest, much pleasure, slave provide contrasts. They work because they are complete opposites of the fear death often evokes.
3. Donne makes us aware of strong religious belief through expressions like "nor yet canst ye kill me," "soul's delivery" and "we wake eternally."
4. Answers may vary.
   Mighty and dreadful, for thou art not.

Answers Successful English 8A

Page 32
Answer the questions

1. Herrick is saying that we grieve to see the daffodil bud waste away so quickly before noon. He begs it stay until the day's end.

2. In the second verse he says that men also have a transient life and even youth does not last long.

3. Answers will vary. Any of the following:
   —the short lived nature of life and the fleeting passage of time.
   —like flowers humans have a very short life in this world.
   —beauty will not remain forever.

4. Herrick refers to a man's youth as spring.

5. Like to the summer's rain
   as the pearls of morning dew
   He used the similes to explain how short is our life.

Page 33
Notes for Debate
   Parent to check.

   At the heart of the problem, King Charles 1 believed in the "Divine Right of Kings." This meant that he believed that his people were subject to his commands without discussion since he was appointed by God as their king. In practise he felt he could levy taxes whenever he wished without recourse to Parliament. He ruled absolutely.

   The Roundheads supported the right of elected officials in Parliament to help govern. They did not believe the king had the right to levy taxes without Parliament's consent.

   In addition their lifestyles were very different. The Cavaliers wore brighter clothing and believed in living life to the full.

   They were also diametrically opposed in matters of religion. The Cavaliers were Catholics, a minority religion in Britain, where most were Anglican. The Roundheads were Puritans and lead a different lifestyle of modest dress and moral behaviour.

Page 34
Figurative language

1. hyperbole
2. simile

Page 35

3. metaphor
4. pun
5. alliteration
6. onomatopoeia
7. pun
8. metaphor
9. alliteration
10. personification
11. hyperbole
12. simile

A. Similes in sentences
   Parent to check. Make sure the child uses more than two or three words.

B. Explain similes
   Answers may vary slightly.
   1. to fight fiercely
   2. to sing beautifully
   3. to fly effortlessly

Page 36
A. Modifies verb, adjective or adverb?
   1. verb
   2. adverb
   3. verb   adjective.
   4. adverb   verb

B. Adverb and type
   1. promptly   time
   2. prematurely   manner
   3. there   place
   4. then   manner
      now   time
   5. here   place
   6. rarely   time
   7. emphatically   manner
   8. immediately   time

Page 37
Word Form
   1. The kitten played mischievously with the wool.
   2. The officer pointed out the direction I was to head in.
   3. He is reputed to be something of a genius at maths.
   4. One can only say that the diplomats were treated deplorably.
   5. With great anticipation the crowd watched as the gymast began her routine.

6. The hostile audience booed the performance.

7. The judge expressed some cynicism at the hardened criminal's repentance.

8. The young golfer spoke sarcastically to his caddy.

9. The air-traffic controller perspired freely as she noticed the plane's sudden deviation from course.

10. A careless approach to marriage has often been identified as an important cause of separation.

11. As the crowd watched, the athlete fell, groaning in agonising pain.

Page 39
A. Word Knowledge
1. jurisdiction
2. endowed
3. assimilated
4. proprietary
5. subordination

B. Answer these questions:
1. Any order

   a meadow from which hay could be mown to feed the oxen

   cattle and sheep kept where there was a larger pasture to give milk, cheese and wool

   woodlands that provided fuel and building material

   pond or stream that provided fish

   mill for grinding corn

   church or chapel

2. A Glebe was the land that was endowed with the church to support the priest. It consisted of strips scattered through the open fields and a share in the meadows, pastures and woods.

3. The lord had jurisdiction over all his estate including the village.

4. Answers may vary.

   The manorial court was the place that the lord dispensed legal and economic decisions after the central government system had disintegrated so it was very important. As the land was divided up into plots in different places there would inevitably have been disputes over their position and the share of crops etc. as well as the sharing of oxen and ploughs.

5. Answers will vary.
   Peasants huts were small, wooden and no doubt built close together. It would therefore be more efficient and safer to have a communal oven. This would likely be separated from the huts in an open spot to prevent fires. It would also require less firewood to run one large oven.

C. Grammar
1. always   frequently   hard
2. most   certain   common   sufficient   adequate

Page 41
A. Answer these questions:
1. Answers may vary. Suggestion:
   When civil dudgeon first grew high,
   And men fell out they knew not why;

2. Answers may vary. Suggestion: He is described satirically because the way he came out (presumably of the castle) and his appearance is exaggerated. Even his horses virtues are mentioned and made fun of.

3. Answers may vary. Suggestions:
   It was probably popular because it made fun of the Civil War, and various religious groups. It was amusing, easy to read and full of wit.

B. Answer questions
1. Nature is personified.

Page 42
2. Answers may vary. Suggestions:
   Nature's face; sweetly smiles; frowns severe; cloudy brow

3. Personifying each season gives us a quick, pictorial reminder of the seasons, e.g., Autumn's...cloudy brow; Summer fruits.

4. alternate lines

Answer these questions
1. Answers will vary. Suggestions:
   darkly wise; rudely great; born die; reasoning but to err; abused disabused;

Answers Successful English 8A

Page 43

2. Man is a complex being. Sometimes he is wise and sometimes foolish. He is born but eventually he dies. He is capable of reasoning but often gets it wrong. He either thinks too well of himself or too ill.

3. He is saying know yourself. There is enough to keep you busy in that without questioning where you are in God's plan.

Page 44
French Words

1. deja vu
2. en route
3. petit four
4. haute coutre
5. matinee
6. protege
7. hors d'oeuvre
8. maître d'
9. par excellence
10. au fait
11. potpourri
12. en suite
13. piece de resistance
14. attaché
15. café au lait
16. cordon bleu
17. faux pas

Page 45

1. a burning question
2. to blow one's own trumpet
3. to turn the other cheek
4. to carry coals to Newcastle
5. to be fond of the limelight
6. to keep someone at arm's length
7. to pick someone's brain
8. to put someone in the picture
9. to set people by the ears
10. that rings a bell
11. a bone of contention
12. cheek by jowl
13. a cuckoo in the nest
14. a second string to one's bow

Page 46
Pronouns

1. you and me personal; your possessive himself reflective:

which relative; him personal; someone indefinite; it personal

2. that demonstrative

3. myself reflexive

Page 47

4. neither indefinite
5. what interrogative you personal
6. that demonstrative
7. themselves reflexive pronoun
8. several indefinite
9. each distributive
10. somebody indefinite
11. it impersonal
12. she personal whom relative
13. this demonstrative hers mine possessive
14. each distributive

Word Knowledge

1. vocabulary
2. tragedy
3. dialogue
4. colloquial
5. summary
6. sympathy
7. unanimous

Page 49
A. Word Knowledge

1. baliff
2. demesne
3. appurtances
4. heriot
5. boon work
6. taille
7. reeve
8. merchet

B. Answer these questions

1. The demesne of the lord compromised a quarter to one third of the arable land.

2. No they did not. A few peasants were free men. Some peasants possessed smaller tenements than others and were of lower social standing.

3. The lord's revenue was made up of the harvest from his land, which if there was excess he could sell; his animals; the money raised by the heriot, merchet and taille.

4. The peasant's welfare was dependent on several things. They were dependent on the goodwill of the lord of the manor or his baliff. If he was fair and his decisions in the manorial court were just then the peasants life would have been easier. If he was greedy or cruel they would have suffered greatly.

Both the lord of the manor and the

© Valerie Marett
Coroneos Publications

Australian Homeschooling #562
Successful English 8A

peasant's welfare was subject to the weather as they depended on the crops for food. Bad crops or illness among the stock could leave them starving.

Page 51
Answer these questions:
1. It is probably England was a metaphor for people in general and Jerusalem was a force of good that would defeat evil.

2. Answers will vary. Parent to check. Suggestion: And was Jerusalem builded here........ satanic mills? Blake might be questioning whether anything good could have been found near such evil places as these mills.

3. The imagery suggests a fight as it describes implements of warfare. That they are gold suggests the fight is for good.

4. The mental fight was with others. It was to be in the form of persuasion. The sword mentioned may have been words, written or said, as this is a common metaphor.

Page 52
Answer these questions
1. Answers will vary. Suggestions: The poet says that he was walking by himself in the country when he encountered a field of daffodils by a lake. They looked so beautiful waving in the breeze that they made him feel happy. He often recalls the memory when he is in bed at night and once again feels happy.

2. Answers will vary. Suggestions: lonely as a cloud; continuous as the stars that shine

3. The personification is almost in a reverse form for the poet compares himself to a cloud floating over the hills.

4. Answers will vary Suggestions: cloud and crowd; trees and breeze

Essay
Parents to check.

Page 53
Insert Proper Noun
1. England
2. March
3. Auckland
4. Atlantic

5. Edison
6. QANTAS
7. Mercury
8. Columbus
9. Nelson
10. Ford
11. Titanic
12. Nile
13. New Guinea
14. Beethoven
15. Everest
16. Italian
17. Easter
18. Queen Elizabeth
19. Tasmania
20. Sarah-Anne
21. igneous
22. Asia

Food Twins
1. apples
2. eggs
3. chips
4. butter
5. cream
6. tomato sauce
7. mint sauce
8. jelly
9. crackers
10. beans
11. spaghetti
12. marmalade

Page 54
Word Knowledge
1. adjourn
2. mitigating
3. pusillanimous
4. monogram
5. allegation
6. evasive
7. matricide
8. buoyant
9. acclimatised
10. recriminations
11. cudgelling
12. despicable
13. insular
14. infantile

Page 55
Form
Parent to correct. Make sure each box is x Yes or No and student understands what the question is asking.

Page 56

A. Underlined preosition

1. paddock—noun governed
   across the paddock—phrase
   we   paddock—relationship

2. man   moon —noun governed
   in the man; in the moon—phrases
   people   man   moon—relationship

3. eye—noun governed
   with the black eye—phrase
   boy   eye—relationship

B. Choose a preposition

1. within
2. for
3. from
4. beneath
5. behind
6. between

C. Correct phrase

1. <u>without</u> counting the cost
2. <u>between</u> two fires
3. <u>within</u> a stone's throw
4. <u>up</u> to the hilt
5. <u>under</u> a cloud

Page 57

Insert correct preposition

1. on
2. with   about
3. from
4. among
5. to
6. of   from
7. with   for or against
8. to   for
9. with
10. into
11. to   against

Page 59

A. Answer the questions:

1. Answers will vary. Suggestion:
   Many towns had some sort of wall which would provide some protection to those inside to barbarian marauders. Many of these invaders did not arrive in large numbers so larger towns, where more people lived, would have been attacked last. In addition, when more people live together, e.g., in a town, there would be more men to fight or attack invaders.

2. The barbarians were used to living in the country and not towns so when they settled, they settled in the country rather than in towns where they felt shut in.

3. Since there was no strong government larger towns were forced to build strong walls and arm themselves with fighting men.

4. allegiance, monetary payment, aid in his war enterprises

5. The three classes in the ninth century were the clergy, the nobles and the peasantry.

6. The fourth class that emerged was the middle class who dwelt in towns and were dependent on commerce.

7. Answers may vary slightly. The towns would be more dependent on trade. Agriculture did not develop as fast so there was little left to send into towns.

B. Word Knowledge

1. corporate
2. counter-part
3. bourgeoisie

Page 61

Answer these questions:

1. alternating Answers will vary: ran, man; ground, round

2. Answers may vary. Yes, they provide a contrast. The rest of the poem paints a picture of beauty and order. The thought of war brings to mind chaos, ugliness and disorder and thereby provides a contrast.

3. Answers will vary: "gardens bright with sinuous rile" contrast with "from this chasm, with ceaseless turmoil seething." (This is a description of a river winding through a chasm to the sea.)

Page 62

Answer these questions:

1. Answers will vary. The theme is that no matter how great or powerful a man is, he will eventually die. OR The theme is that over time things change.

2. The statement by Ramses has been sandwiched between the description of a broken statue and a picture of nothing else but endless sand showing irony of Ramses statement.
   It is also ironic that it is not anything of the

Answers Successful English 8A

king that remains but something of the sculptor in the remanent of the statue he made.

3. Answers may vary. vast, trunkless legs; shattered visage; colossal wreck; lone and level sands.

Page 63
Answer these questions:
1. His examples include the sun, moon, flowers, people, daffodils, streams, musk-rose blooms, and any lovely tale we have heard or read.
2. "Simple sheep" is a metaphor for human innocence.
3. The poet says that beautiful things lift our spirits and give us joy for ever.

Page 64
Ambiguity
1. The lawyer, from a distant town, harangued the jury.
2. For Sale: a house for $100,000. At this price the house will soon sell so contact us now.
3. I like Luna Park more than my girlfriend does.
4. For the experience of a lifetime drink GoGo energy drink. You'll never get a better drink.
5. When the car hit the truck the truck's load shifted and pinned the lower half of the truck driver's body. The load had to be removed to free him.
6. The buyer was able to get a special deal on the car as it was something of a wreck.
7. The boy, with a very odd look, emerged from the house.
8. Australians like potatoes, mashed or not mashed.
9. Well pleased with his day's work, he took the bull home.
10. The jug, which was fortunately empty, hit him on the head.

Page 65
Knowledge of nouns
1. a. directory
   b. inventory
   c. catalogue

2. a. haulier
   b. courier
3. a. experiment
   b. inspection
   c. inquest
4. a. scabbard
   b. phial
   c. quiver
5. a. prologue
   b. preface
   c. preamble

Page 66
Identify the sentence
1. response—greeting

Page 67
2. response to a conventional greeting
3. direct question
4. response that indicates the listener disagrees
5. statement that communicates an observation.
6. command to elicit a direct answer
7. command eliciting a decision to act.
8. Statement communicating a judgement
9. question that expresses doubt
10. response that indicates the listener is paying attention
11. exclamation
12. response or answer not in the form of a normal statement or exclamation
13. rhetorical statement
14. communication by inference
15. response indicating listener agrees

Page 68
A. Use conjunction to complete sentence
1. Andrew was unsuccessful because he wasted so much time.

2. They arrived while I was still eating breakfast.

3. I can not buy a bicycle until I have saved more money.

4. Nearly a month has passed since I received your letters.

5. John will play if you will play too.

B. Complete with a conjunction
1. since
2. Although
3. before   or after

C. Underline conjunction
1. and
2. but
3. when
4. in order to   and

Page 69
Choosing the right word
1. incredible
2. morale
3. voracious
4. gamble
5. illicit
6. exceed
7. adversity
8. sole
9. sight
10. veracious
11. moral
12. incredulous
13. adversary
14. accede
15. site
16. soul
17. vacation

Page 71
Answer these questions
1. The earliest trade centres sprang up in areas where agricultural production didn't produce enough for the population.

2. Luxury trade played a greater part in the Mediterranean as there was sea access to the East. In the north access was along a hazardous route. Those in the north also had to pay tolls to feudal lords along the way and risked having their merchandise confiscated if the lord was short of money. In the Mediterranean risks were less and the route more direct.

3. It was the revival of commerce that led to the revival of towns because no trade route could exist without places to stop for a short time and to sell their goods or else a base to work from. Conversely no town could exist unless they were on trade routes as they needed the goods the trade route brought to them.

4. Merchants needed:
   a. base of operations strategically situated along trade routes, local markets that wanted their goods and places that provided warehousing, shipping and/or transport.
   b. Merchants needed security in the form of protection from strong, local feudal lords against war or seizure of goods by other lords.
   c. Merchants required freedom of movement and freedom from restrictions of the manorial peasantry.

5. outside fortified   new walls to surround enveloped

6. The town wall showed where the town ended and where the country began. It also showed that they were independent of the manor.

Page 74
Answer these questions
1. The verses vary in length from six to twelve lines.

2. "Flashed all their sabres bare/ Flashed as they turned in air/ Sab'ring the gunmen there." or
"Cannon to the right of them/ Cannon to the left of them/ Cannon in front of them."
Both of these leave the reader with a sense of unrelenting assault.

3. Answers will vary.
   Suggestions: Britain was not doing well in the war in the Crimea. It is possible that Alfred, Lord Tennyson wrote this poem to lift the spirits of the British by emphasising that even against fearful odds the British do not give up. He definitely wrote it to extol the bravery of the men who died.

Page 76
Answer these questions:
1a. postern: a secondary gate in the fortification of a city wall

   b. a strap encircling a horse's body in order to secure a saddle.

   c. froth at the mouth showing the horses were pushed hard

   d. head over heels; literally head over rump

   e. leather coat worn as protection from the weather

2. Answers may vary slightly.
   In verse three Browning initially tells us

that the rider started his ride while the moon was in the sky. He then takes us through various changes in the sky as the sun rises and moves slowly overhead. This gives us the feeling that considerable time is passing.

3. The other two riders were Dirck and Joris. The riders' horses died under them because they had been pushed so hard.

4. The storyteller's horse was called Roland.

5. He threw away as much as he could so that he could lighten the load for his horse to ensure it didn't die and the message reached Aix.

Further Work

Parent to check. It is suggested the children in this village may have died in the plague or they may have been lured away in the "Children's Crusade" in 1212.

Page 77
Correct word in correct place

1. negligent   negligible
2. intricate   extricate
3. beneficent   beneficial
4. punctual   punctilious
5. continually   continuously
6. paramount   tantamount
7. deprecated   depreciated
8. explicit   implicit
9. ostensible   ostentatious
10. adept   adapt

Page 79
Important Definitions

1. anticlimax
2. couplet
3. alliteration
4. epigram
5. spoonerism
6. irony
7. epitaph
8. antithesis
9. cliché
10. fable
11. epitaph

Page 80
Subject & Predicate

1. they—subject
   how do   make poetry—predicate

2. John—subject
   threw the ball over my head—predicate

3. a runaway pony—subject
   galloped round the corner

4. You—assumed subject
   come quickly—predicate

5. the man—subject
   came to our rescue—predicate
   we—subject
   asked for help—predicate

6. Dawn Fraser—subject
   what   was an extraordinary athlete—predicate

7. My brother—subject
   shaves—predicate
   he—subject
   he gets up in the morning   when—predicate

8. Someone—subject
   has purposely removed it—predicate

9. I—subject
   shall go —predicate
   it—subject
   providing   is fine—predicate

Page 81
Subject, Predicate, Object

1. that boy—subject
   likes brown sugar—predicate
   sugar—object

2. He—subject
   calls the tune—predicate
   object—tune
   he (understood)—subject
   who **pays** the piper—predicate
   piper—object

3. Men with beards—subject
   have many female admirers—predicate
   admirers—object

4. The girl—subject
   won a university scholarship—predicate
   a university scholarship—object
   the girl (understood)—subject
   who **lives** there   —predicate

5. They—subject
   disguised themselves—predicate
   themselves—object
   they—subject

   so   **should** not **be recognised**—predicate

6. His sister—subject

mended his trousers with great skill—
predicate
trousers—object

7. Roger—subject
finished his homework—predicate
homework—object
his homework (understood)—subject
set by his teacher—predicate
teacher—object

8. Anyone—subject
did see anything —predicate
anything—object

Page 83
A. Answer these questions:

1. Originally the lords considered the towns to be a source of money when they were running short.

2. Changes were caused by the towns strengthening their walls, defying their lords and shutting their gates against the tax collectors or even the lords. Changes were also caused by the merchants banding together making it harder for the lords to enforce extractions and control movement and sale of goods.

3. The charters contained a guarantee from the lord that anyone who had lived within a town for a year and a day was considered a free person. It granted the right to buy, sell or lease land within the town. It exempted the townspeople from labour services owed by the peasants. Money was paid in purchasing the charter instead of paying rent to the lord. Finally they had the right to sue or be sued in the urban court instead of taking it to the lord's court.

4. Lords who granted these charters benefitted from the money they received from the purchase of the charters and the increased profit from their manor because of the growing market in the towns for agricultural products.

5. As the towns grew in strength they eventually threw off their

dependence on the lord or king and became virtual independent states.

B. Word Knowledge

1. bourgeois
2. enfranchisement
3. franchises

C. Grammar
towns—subject
were the wealthiest member of the feudal system—predicate
members—object

Page 84
Answer the questions:
1. couplets
2. personified
3. The only things moving are the moon and a small mouse. This gives the poem a slow moving, soft, still feeling.

Page 85
4. The moon's beams make the world appear silver and fairy-like.

Page 86
1. Answers may differ slightly. There are fifty nine swans. The swans have not grown weary over the nineteen years, even though he, (Yeats,) has. They remain faithful to their partners—swans mate for life. They padde as friends together and they fly together. They are mysterious and beautiful.

2. Nature: Yeats describes the beauty of nature and its continuity.

   Aging: Yeats feels he is aging and losing the energy and love of life that the swans possess.

   Immortality or Permanence: the swans represent immortality and their passion, desire for success and beauty will last. The passing of time does not cause them to fade.

Page 87
Malapropisms
1. debut
2. vacated
3. prodigy
4. pinnacle
5. optimist
6. emphatic
7. invention
8. exhort sportsmanship
9. forceps
10. credible
11. masticate
12. bannister

Answers Successful English 8A

Page 88
Main and Subordinate Clause

1. **main clause:** the car was fifteen years old
   subordinate clause: that broke down on the freeway

2. **main clause:** he missed the opening speech
   subordinate clause: since he was so late

3. **main clause:** my sister and I were at Grandma's house
   subordinate clause: when my mother rang me to come and collect her.

4. **main clause:** I like to eat lunch outside
   subordinate clause: when the sun is shining.

Page 89

5. **main clause:** Mr Johnson rides the bus to work
   subordinate clause: since his car broke down.

6. **main clauses:** the mouse ran through the kitchen
   (the mouse) ate the bread
   subordinate clause: while the family slept

7. **main clause:** we will play Monopoly this afternoon
   subordinate clause: unless you have another idea

8. **main clause:** magicians often perform tricks
   subordinate clause: which (the tricks) seem impossible

9. **main clause:** pets act obediently
   subordinate clause: who (the pets) are properly trained

10. **main clause:** Mandy cooked a casserole
    subordinate clause: which (the casserole) was delicious

11. **main clause:** David paid the bill
    subordinate clause: after eating his meal

12. **main clause:** John caught the fish
    subordinate clause: Kelly caught one also

Page 91
A. Answer these questions

1. The purpose of the merchant guilds was to preserve a monopoly of all trades for themselves; to give them the strength to bargain with kings and lords, especially when it came to lending money and to control the major positions in the town, e.g., town councillors; to control fairs and dictate the terms on which people could trade with the town.

2. The purpose of craft guilds was to make sure that the merchants treated them fairly and establish standards for each craft and prices for goods sold.

3. Masters were experienced in their trade, owned their own home and had a shop where they sold the goods that were made. Apprentices were people who were learning the trade and who were tied to the master for seven years. Instead of wages they received their food, clothes and board. Journeymen were people who had finished their apprenticeship and were free to work for themselves.

4. Before a journeyman could become a master he had to submit a piece of work, known as a "master-piece" to the guild inspectors to be assessed.

B. Word Knowledge
1. monopoly
2. ousting

C. Clauses
Main clause: Masters owned homes
Subordinate clause: (masters) sold goods there

Page 92
Answer the question:

1. Brooke is saying that if he dies, since he grew up in England, part of where he is buried will become part of England. He suggests that the ground that he died on would be made better because of the patriotism of a man who died for his country.

2. This type of short poem is called a sonnet.

Page 94
1. Answers will vary. Suggestions. No, men did not want to fight as is shown the second verse but they could not ignore what was wrong. Verse 4 shows that when war was inevitable patriotism drove them to fight for what they believed was right.

Answers Successful English 8A

2. This line may refer to the fear that people felt as they saw their men leave to fight or it may refer to the fact that many died on the battle ground and left behind family who, despite their grief needed to go on with day to day life.

Further Work
Parent to check.

Page 95
Latin Prefixes
1. antediluvian
2. avert
3. erudite
4. decrepit
5. circumlocution
6. discursive
7. disseminate
8. disingenuous
9. excoriate
10. expulsion
11. intransigent
12. exculpate
13. recondite
14. omnivorous
15. incursion
16. omnipotent
17. permeate
18. preamble

Page 96
Use one word only
1. My uncle is an octogenarian.
2. Frogs are amphibious.
3. He holds a sinecure.
4. After pneumonia he is now convalescent.
5. This event occurs biennially.
6. The artist is an expert at making silhouettes.
7. Mr Jones died intestate.
8. Can you substantiate your claim?
9. In this country there are not many insolvent tradesmen.
10. The body was exhumed.
11. The chairman ruled that the point raised was irrelevant.

Page 97
1. Help me put away the crockery.
2. The weather is unexpected.
3. Deciduous trees lose their leaves in winter.
4. He spoke crossly.
5. The ball landed on the course.
6. Always answer emails immediately.
7. The old man looked ecstatic.

Page 98
Figures of Speech
1. We are two men in the same boat.
2. He is rotten to the core.
3. It makes my flesh creep.

Page 99
A. Which has a metaphor?
1. The disappointment broke her heart.
2. At the slightest difficulty Janet flies to her mother.
3. The minutes crept slowly by.

B.
Similes to metaphors
1. My heart was in my mouth.
2. You have put the cart before the horse.
3. We are flogging a dead horse.

C. Personification, hyperbole, pun, epigram, onomatopoeia, alliteration, metaphor or simile?
1. epigram
2. alliteration
3. personification
4. metaphor
5. pun
6. onomatopoeia
7. hyperbole
8. simile
9. metaphor

Page 100
Adjectival clause
1. where the plays are performed (clause)
   place—noun modified
2. when Alice was married (clause)
   year—noun modified
3. that he entered (clause)
   moment—noun modified
4. whose cat you found (clause)
   boy—noun modified
5. that you bought (clause)
   dress—noun modified
6. who was standing beside you (clause)
   girl—noun modified
7. which meets on Thursday (clause)
   class—noun modified

© Valerie Marett
Coroneos Publications

Australian Homeschooling #562
Successful English 8A

8. which was selected (clause)
   flower—noun modified

9. whom you helped (clause)
   friend—noun modified

Page 101
A. Combine sentences into a clause

1. A wren, that had been injured, was trying to build its nest.

2. This is the building where I go to school.

3. Aunty Pauline is my mother's sister who will visit us in June.

4. Do you remember the name of the man whom you met?

5. She is the one who thought of the idea.

B. Adjectival and main clause

1. that you like (adj. clause)
   Tammy likes the same books (main clause)

2. who wishes to leave early (adj. clause)
   Anyone may do so. (main clause)

3. whose wife teaches English (adj. clause)
   The man is a tennis professional.

4. to whom I would entrust a secret (adj. clause)
   He is not the sort of man. (main clause)

5. (that) I was telling you about (adj. clause)
   This is the book. (main clause.)

C. Add a main clause

Answers will vary. Parent to check. Suggestions below:

1. Janet, who called a few minutes ago, has been delayed.

2. We will know who won the Cup when the results are announced.

Page 103
A. Word Knowledge

1. impetus
2. usury
3. capitalism
4. cosmopolitan

B. Answer these questions

1. A few towns managed to gain political power by banding together in a "commune" or sworn political alliance.

2. Those with the greatest political power were largely in Italy.

3. The larger towns in Italy were ideally placed to trade with the East, where many other European towns were not so strategically placed. The Italian towns trade was also stimulated by the Crusades. (The Pope lived in Italy and most European armies came through Italy to gain his blessing. Italy also provided a good jumping off spot to the Holy Land.)

4. Milan, Florence, Genoa, Pisa, Venice.

5. Many of towns democratic institutions were overthrown and fell into the hands of local despots.

6. The Jews were left to run the banking system because the Catholic Church forbad the loaning of money at interest. The Jews, not being part of the Catholic Church, were under no such prohibition and therefore took on the job.

   The Jews were hated because they became wealthy through running the banking.

7. The banks accepted deposits, arranged for money to be transferred to other accounts in payment of commercial debt, allowed customers to overdraw their accounts (lines of credit) and eventually even arranged for "bills of exchange" which meant that there was no need for the transport of gold from place to place with the danger of robbery.

Page 104

1. Both England, Death and Night have been personified.

Page 105

2. England has been personified as a mother who mourns for her dead and in the last verse as knowing her dead and keeping them in her heart for ever. Death has been personified as royalty—note such words as august, royal, immortal. Night has been

described as a person who knows the stars.

3. The imagery is of youth and courage. The youth of those going to fight is portrayed in their straight limbs, true eye. Their courage is portrayed in their steady, unflinching glance, their courage to the end and the fact that they fell facing the foe and not running away.

Page 106

1. The thunder of guns is likened to the rumbling of thunder during a storm. The author has used a simile.

2. Answers may vary. The gunner is a partner with his guns as he has to sight, load and fire them and neither can function separately.

3. The metaphors are "the Sands of Time" and the "Gods of War."

4. Answers may vary. Troops under fire must have considered the firing of their own guns music and it was obviously music to the gunners.

5. It is written in capital letters and repeated to emphasise the noise of the guns.

Page 107

Answers will vary. Suggestions. No man can afford to turn a blind eye to what is wrong or we should stand together when something wrong occurs and not think it does not affect us.

Page 108
Holocaust

Answers will vary. Suggestion: that the deaths in the Holocaust were not just numbers. They were real people and many of them were children who died far too early.

Which Poet or Age was best

Answers will vary. Parent to check. Make sure that a reasoned argument is given and not just "I liked …….. best."

Revision

Page 109
Review—Nouns
A. Collective nouns
   1. library
   2. bouquet

3. fleet
4. pack
5. set
6. flight
7. swarm
8. pack

B. Small quantity
   1. ounce
   2. blade
   3. splinter
   4. drop

C. Abstract Noun
   1. decision
   2. surliness
   3. i solation
   4. repentance
   5. explosion
   6. eruption

D. Abstract noun for definition
   1. courage
   2. gratefulness
   3. fellowship
   4. persuasion

E. Neuter Gender
   Parent to check.
   Examples: house, grass, lake, pen

F. Common Gender
   Any order
   people, poultry, children, sheep
   you, we, us, they, them

Page 110
A. Correct Word
   1. allusion
   2. affect
   3. mien
   4. stationary
   5. contemptible

B. Occupation
   1. mason
   2. steeplejack
   3. chauffeur
   4. glazier
   5. confectioner

C. Complete Sentence
   1. secede
   2. artillery
   3. testify

4. vacancy
5. democracy   bureaucracy
6. intercede
7. succeed   bribery
8. ecstasy

Page 111
A. Transitive or intransitive
1. sang (v) transitive
2. were (v) transitive
3. laughed (v) intransitive

B. Verb and tense
1. noticed   past tense
2. says   present tense
3. will be deserted   future tense

C. Nouns and verbs
1. explorers; cabin; repair (nouns)
   reached; was (verbs)
2. I; I; John (nouns)
   trust; trusted (verbs)
3. Aunt Debbie; meal; restaurant (nouns)
   knows; are served (verbs)
4. she; she; others (nouns)
   ran; overtook (verbs)
5. I; train (nouns)
   is raining; catch (verbs)

Page 112
French Phrases
1. sabotage
2. debut
3. facade
4. premiere
5. non de plume
6. tete-a-tete
7. vinaigrette
8. au fait
9. resume
10. a la carte
11. applique
12. fait accompli
13. boutique
14. bon appetite
15. repertoire
16. a la mode

Page 113
A. Type of Adjective, Noun Qualified
1. this: demonstrative cake (n)
   cream: descriptive   cake (n)
2. neither: distributive girl (n)
   which: interrogative way (n)
3. hardest, last: descriptive day (n)
   sixth: numerical day (n) (understood)

4. My: possessive   cat (n)
   that: demonstrative   dog (n)

B. Change to an adjective
1. The sky was lowering.
2. Business men usually look spruce.

C. Replace with Adjective
1. lowering
2. spruce
3. A good guard has to be vigilant.
4. The explorer came to an impenetrable
   mountain.
5. The visitor was unceremonious.
6. The room looked squalid.

Page 114
Figures of Speech
1. hyperbole
2. pun
3. onomatopoeia
4. simile
5. personification
6. alliteration
7. metaphor
8. pun
9. personification
10. hyperbole
11. metaphor
12. alliteration
13. simile
14. onomatopoeia
15. personification
16. onomatopoeia
17. alliteration
18. hyperbole
19. metaphor

Page 115
A. What does it modify?
1. adjective
2. adjective
3. adverb
4. verb
5. adjective
6. adverb

B. Adverb: manner, time or place
1. quietly   manner
2. tomorrow   time
3. here   place
4. near   place
5. easily   manner
6. yesterday   early   time
7. still   time
8. behind   place

Answers Successful English 8A

9. carefully manner
10. later time
11. rarely time
12 loudly manner

Page 116
French Words
1. haute coutre
2. maître d'
3. piece de resistance
4. deja vu
5. faux pas
6. en route
7. café au lait
8. potpourii
9. hors d'oeuvre
10. petit four
11. protégé
12. attache
13. cordon bleu
14. par excellence
15. matinee
16. en suite
17. au fait

Page 117
Common Figurative Expressions
1. a second string to one's bow
2. to turn the other cheek
3. to pick someone's brain
4. a bone of contention
5. a burning question
6. to keep someone at arm's length
7. a cuckoo in the nest
8. to blow one's trumpet
9. to be fond of the limelight
10. to put someone in the picture
11. to carry coal to Newcastle
12. that rings a bell
13. cheek by jowl
14. to set people by the ears

Page 1118
Pronouns
1. neither distributive
2. it impersonal
3. I personal
4. none indefinite these demonstrative
5. himself reflexive
6. its personal
7. that demonstrative
8. several indefinite us personal
9. who relative
10. what interrogative
    your personal

11. which relative mine possessive
12. this that demonstrative
13. myself reflexive
14. someone distributive
15. he personal
16. it impersonal
17. everything indefinite
    he personal
18. whose relative
    this impersonal

Page 119
Prepositions
1. girls; hair—noun governed
   of girls; with short hair—phrase
   grandfather girls hair—relationship

2. one (parcel understood)—
   noun- governed
   from the last one—phrase
   parcel one—relationship

3. colour—noun governed
   in colour—phrase
   television colour—relationship

4. room—noun governed
   in the next room—phrase
   he room—relationship

B. Correct Preposition for Use
1. for to
2. among between
3. to
4. into
5. with
6. against (could also be for)
7. with
8. for
9. about
10. to

Page 120
Ambiguity
1. Wearing his best clothes the young child entered the room that had just been painted.

2. My friend said that, falling asleep I began to talk aloud as I dreamed.

3. Professor Bright, of the University of Western Australia, has been doing research on human behaviour.

4. I remember, as a boy, emptying my money-box to buy a number of white mice.

5. Try our hot pies! You'll never taste better pies.

© Valerie Marett
Coroneos Publications

Australian Homeschooling #562
Successful English 8A

Answers Successful English 8A

6. He had no intention of insulting her.

7. The teacher, in a loud voice, told him to be quiet.

8. He was angry with his brothers, especially James, for blaming his children.

9. Not long afterwards came the potato famine and the potato was, of course, the Irishman's staple diet.

Page 121
Identify Sentences

1. Greeting

2. response to a conventional greeting

3. statement that may communicate an inference

4. command that seeks to stimulate direct action

5. question that may express doubt

6. exclamation

7. response that indicates the listener agrees

8. statement that seeks unreasoning acceptance of judgement

9. rhetorical question

10. response or answer not in the usual form of statement

11. command that may invite a decision to act.

Page 122
Subject, Predicate, Object

1. Mark and I—subject
   played basketball—predicate
   basketball—object

2. Reading and learning—subject
   can be fun activities—predicate
   activities—object

3. you—subject
   do **want to eat** pasta or pizza—predicate
   pasta or pizza—object

4. I—subject
   read a book—predicate
   book—object
   I (understood)—subject
   ate a box of chocolates—predicate
   chocolates—object

5. John, Mark, Jacob and Luke—subject
   ate waffles—predicate
   waffles—object

6. Frank—subject
   ate waffles, bacon, toast and potatoes—predicate
   waffles, bacon, toast, potatoes—object

7. Doug and David—subject
   washed and **waxed** the car—predicate
   car—object

8. My Mum—subject
   told me—predicate
   me—object
   Your sister—subject
   is at the park—predicate
   park—object

9. I—subject
   rode my bike—predicate
   bike—object

10. Tennis and football—subject
    are both popular sports—predicate
    sports—object

Page 123
Important Definitions

1. antithesis
2. spoonerism
3. irony
4. cliché
5. anticlimax
6. couplet
7. alliteration
8. epitaph
9. epigram
10. fable

Page 124
Main and Subordinate clauses

1. Main clause: Krystal will be late for music practise
   Subordinate clause: if she goes to the shops

2. Main clause: Adam received a football
   Subordinate clause: which he traded for a cricket bat.

3. Main clause: We were watching TV on the couch
   Subordinate clause: and (we were) eating sandwiches

4. Main clause: Kim likes listening to her iPod
   Subordinate clause: which (the iPod) is pink.

5. Main clause: The dog barked at the burglar
   Subordinate clause: who was stealing the computer

6. Main clause: she has joined a pony club
   Subordinate clause: since Suzanne likes to ride horses.

Page 125
Malapropisms

1. proceed
2. punctual
3. evacuate
4. photographic
5. crustaceans
6. moss
7. influence
8. circumnavigate
9. bated
10. dissension
11. stature
12. contradiction
13. voracious
14. fait accompli
15. prostrate
16. equilateral

Page 126
Words Using Latin Prefix

1. circumlocution
2. expulsion
3. omnipotent
4. antediluvian
5. intransigent
6. avert
7. incursion
8. recondite
9. decrepit
10. disseminate
11. discursive
12. disingenuous
13. omnivorous
14. permeate
15. excoriate
16. exculpate
17. preamble
18. erudite

Page 127
Using One Word For Many

1. intestate
2. maritime
3. hostage
4. immaterial
5. ambiguous
6. rhetoric

7. procrastination
8. infallibility
9. impecunious
10. innocuous
11. impermeable

Page 128
A. Simile to metaphor

1. Whatever I said went in one ear and out another.

2. She is tied to her mother's apron strings.

3. Her heart is made of gold.

B. Personification, hyperbole, pun, epigram, onomatopoeia, alliteration, metaphor or simile?

1. hyperbole
2. personification
3. pun
4. alliteration
5. simile
6. metaphor
7. epigram
8. onomatopoeia
9. euphemism
10. hyperbole
11. personification

Page 129
A. Adjectival Clause

1. which Jane mentioned (adj. clause)
   city (noun)

2. that I saw (adj. clause)
   man (noun)

3. that followed the thunderstorm (adj. clause)
   weather (noun)

4. when acting auditions will be held (adj. clause)
   time period (noun)

B. Combining sentences to make an adjectival clause

1. The woman, who lives next door, is a registered nurse.

2. Summer, which is my favourite season, starts next week.

3. The dog that you found belongs to the Smiths.
4. This is the building where I learn dancing.

C. Adjectival & Main Clause

1. (that) I picked out for you (adj. clause)
   How do you like the flavour?

(main clause)

2. which dates back to Roman times (adj. clause)
Unlike the organ the piano is fairly modern. (main clause)

3. whom I have known for twenty years (adj. clause)
Mary is leaving the district (main clause)